英语专业
系列教材

English Writing Workbook

英语写作实践教程

（第二版）

李贵苍 主编

熊金才 朱嫣然 付安权 编写

清华大学出版社

北京

内 容 简 介

本教程基于编者多年的教学实践编写而成,内容涉及英语基础写作的主要方面,如写作障碍、写作过程、选词方法、主题句写作、定义法、比较对照法、分类法等。在课时计算、内容布局、上课步骤、课内读写练习、小组讨论、优秀作文展示、教师讲评、学生意见反馈等环节都力求做到逻辑严密、多寡得当、难易适度,并留给教学双方充分的选择余地。多年的教学效果表明,该教程不仅有助于学生掌握基本的写作知识,提高写作能力,也有利于培养学生的组织表达能力、协作能力、独立思考问题的能力、思辨能力及适应工作的能力,使学生能够满足社会需求。

本教程适于大专院校英语专业学生及英语写作爱好者使用。

图书在版编目(CIP)数据

英语写作实践教程/李贵苍主编;熊金才,朱嫣然,付安权编写. —2 版. —北京:清华大学出版社,2012(2024.7 重印)
英语专业系列教材
ISBN 978-7-302-29921-9

Ⅰ. ①英… Ⅱ. ①李… ②熊… ③朱… ④付… Ⅲ. ①英语-写作-高等学校-教材 Ⅳ. ①H315

中国版本图书馆 CIP 数据核字(2012)第 202643 号

责任编辑:蔡心奕
封面设计:常雪影
责任校对:王荣静
责任印制:杨 艳

出版发行:清华大学出版社
  网 址:https://www.tup.com.cn, https://www.wqxuetang.com
  地 址:北京清华大学学研大厦 A 座   邮 编:100084
  社 总 机:010-83470000   邮 购:010-62786544
  投稿与读者服务:010-62776969, c-service@tup.tsinghua.edu.cn
  质量反馈:010-62772015, zhiliang@tup.tsinghua.edu.cn
印 装 者:三河市人民印务有限公司
经 销:全国新华书店
开 本:185mm×230mm   印 张:15.75   字 数:310 千字
版 次:2009 年 4 月第 1 版 2013 年 2 月第 2 版 印 次:2024 年 7 月第 8 次印刷
定 价:59.00 元

产品编号:047073-04

第二版前言

　　"写作"不仅是英语专业学生的必修课,而且是人们知识建构过程中必不可少的和最重要的一个环节,同时也是人们建构自我的必要手段和最佳途径之一。外语能力大致分为两类:输入性能力和输出性能力。前者涵盖外语学习过程中体现出来的各种学习外语的能力,如记忆单词、阅读文本、练习听力等,而后者主要体现为外显的和使用外语的能力,如口语和书面语表达的能力。如果说,提高输入性能力的目的是彰显输出性能力,那么,外语学习的目标就是尽量使这两类能力达到高度统一,而最能体现这种统一的就是外语写作能力。

　　为什么说"写作"是学习过程中最重要的一个环节呢?这是因为,除了写作,文科学习大多是被动的。不论是在课前预习、课堂听讲、完成作业,还是在课后复习等教学环节中,学生都是被动的,这也是由学习的本质决定的。那么,根据自己的兴趣有选择地大量阅读课外书籍,获取必要的书本知识,丰富自己的阅历,强化自己的知识基础,甚至通过阅读改变自己的知识结构,这些貌似"主动"的获取,是否就是积极主动的学习呢?也不尽然。大凡阅读活动,不论是为了完成课程任务还是出于自己的兴趣爱好,都毫无例外的是一种被动的学习状态,只是"被动"的程度不同而已。这是因为,第一,一旦我们确定了阅读的书目,阅读的内容就已经确定或者给定,不容我们改变;第二,内容的呈现方式是作者从一个特定的视角或者意识形态结构或者特定的社会话语结构中实现的。换句话说,我们所阅读的文本都是作者对社会生活"文化化了"的阐释或者是对个体经验的特殊描写,我们所阅读的无非是某个作者对现实生活的"理解"和"观察"后形成的文字文本,而不是纯粹客观真实的再现。何况,任何"再现"都是经过作者"审美"过了的。第三,阅读的文本是原作者的思想、观察、人生感悟、人生智慧,甚至是乏味的说教文字的再现,带着作者不可克服的局限和偏见。(这当然包括本书的编写者在内。)读者即使能够背诵一篇文章,该篇文章仍然不完全是读者的。即便读者可以对文本中的思想观点提出异议,读者的反应还是受制于原作者的思想和观点,而不完全是发自读者内心的。严肃的读者即使与文本展开激烈的对话,那也是在作者不在场的情形下实现的。读者的思考和反应是在作者的思想基础上的再思考,不完全是读者独立思考的结果。读者即使完全领会了作者的思想和观点,读者仍然是一个读者。这就是为什么只有伟大的作者,而没有伟大的读者的原因。

怎样才是真正的主动学习呢?答案是通过写作。只有当我们开始写作的时候,我们才开始变成真正的自己,才开始走出其他作者的影子,才开始主宰自己的学习,才开始建构自己的文化自我和社会自我,才有可能让历史上和健在的作者服务于我们,即所谓的旁征博引,为我们表现自我、建构自我的写作活动提供一点历史的厚重。

写作的过程就是完善自己的思想和观点的过程,同时也是赋予自己的思想以文字形态的过程,是一个全新的创造的过程。写作并不是仅仅记录下来自己思想的火花,严肃的写作是升华和发展自己思想的过程。这一过程同时也是思考、辨析、批判、反思、对比、深化、修正自己思想的过程,是不断走向自己思想和心灵深处的过程,是与自己灵魂对话的艰难过程,因而也是建构和实现自我的过程。

人类的历史和社会现实都是由语言建构的。离开了语言,我们将无法把握和建构现实,也无法建构自己的存在。瞬息万变的社会生活庞杂、混乱、绵绵不断、无始无终,只有通过写作我们才能给"混乱"以秩序,才能对纷杂的社会万象有所把握,才能给我们飘忽不定的"自我"以方向。正如培根所说,写作使人严谨、准确,只有通过不断的写作,我们才能够更准确地建构自我和把握社会现实。

鲁迅曾经拒绝给年轻的作者开出写作的秘方,因为他不相信写作有什么诀窍。其实,写作的诀窍就是不断写作。我们也并不期望任何仅仅使用这本教程的读者能够一夜成名,像从灰烬中升空的凤凰,变成举世瞩目的作家。但是,我们确信,使用这本写作教程能够使读者获得基本的英语写作技能,能够了解英语不同文体的基本结构和写作方法,并使用这些方法认识自己、表达自己的思想和情感。这本教程的作者多年来一直教授英语写作(其中一位在美国大学多次教授英语写作),了解学生在写作课程上的困惑和需求,因此,新颖性、丰富性、可操作性和实用性始终是这本教程的编写宗旨。

编写完最后一章,经过反复斟酌和比较,我们认为,与同类教材相比,本教程具有以下 8 个鲜明的特征:

1. 适用对象的广泛性。本教程内容丰富多样,既适用于英语专业的学生,也适用于非英语专业的学生和广大的英语爱好者。教程中精选的多篇不同文体的范文,相信能够满足学生不同的需求。

2. 内容的新颖性、创造性和实用性。本教程内容涵盖英语写作的各主要方面,如写作障碍、写作过程、选词方法、主题句写作、段落写作、定义法、比较对照法、分类法、说明解释、主张说服、形容描述、纪事叙述、推论与论证、简历信件等。新颖性主要体现在范文的时代性和适用性;创造性主要体现在学生课堂活动的多样性;实用性主要体现在任务型教学环节的安排和解决具体问题的可操作性方面。

3. 教学理念的先进性。本教程的编写目的是培养学生的创造性和批判性思维能力，有效得体地使用语言的能力和交际能力，坚持以学生为中心的理念，为学生提供充分的自由发挥空间，并以写作为平台，将训练听说读写的能力融于一体。本教程的每节课都设计了学生二人讨论、小组讨论或全班讨论等练习，不仅为学生提供交流思想的机会，而且搭建了一个英语听说的平台。

4. 教学过程的可操作性。本教程是基于编者多年的教学实践而编写的，在课时计算、内容布局、上课步骤、课内读写练习、小组讨论、优秀作文展示、教师讲评、学生意见反馈等环节都力求做到逻辑严密、多寡得当、难易适度，并留给教学双方充分的选择余地。

5. 语言技能的兼容性。本教程注重写作技能与阅读及口语技能的有机结合，使读、写、说等语言能力相得益彰、全面提高。每单元以阅读相关范文开始并以阅读相关范文结束，其中既有精读也有泛读，其间融入教师讲解、写作练习、小组讨论、教师讲评及优秀作文分享，从而保障了学生写与说的时间。

6. 语言知识的丰富性。本教程注重基础语言知识、社会语言知识和相关应用知识的结合。在基础语言知识方面，包括选词知识和篇章结构的知识；在社会语言知识方面，包括文化知识和对策能力；在应用知识方面，重视选材的多学科性、实用性和时代性。

7. 教学活动的多样性。每一单元的写作课都设计了形式多样、内容丰富并与相关主题紧密联系的活动。如范文阅读和讨论（分组讨论范文内容）、教师讲解、写作练习、分组活动、范文展示等。同时还安排了适度的课外写作与阅读练习。

8. 教学效果的显著性。经过多年的教学实践的检验，本教材不仅有助于学生掌握英语的写作知识和技巧，提高写作能力，也有利于培养学生的组织表达能力、协作能力、独立思考问题的能力、思辨能力及适应工作的能力。自使用本教材后，我校英语专业的四、八级考试通过率始终高出全国综合性大学平均通过率 40 个百分点以上，其中写作部分的优势最为明显。

感谢浙江师范大学和清华大学出版社的大力支持，使这本教材得以早日面世。浙江师范大学英语专业被评为浙江省优势专业，教材建设是其中的一项重要内容，我们这次对第一版教材做了比较大的改动：增加了"修辞与写作"、"论文写作"和"MLA 格式"三章，删除了对英语专业学生不太实用的"看图作文"一章，并对全书重新做了一次全面的审校。我们要特别感谢本教材的匿名评审专家，其严谨的学风和渊博的知识更好地保证了本教材的质量。本教材的责任编辑和编辑室的其他同志，不仅具有独到的眼光和热忱，而且付出了辛勤的劳动。在此，我们表示由衷的谢忱。

2012 年 8 月于浙江师范大学

CONTENTS

目　录

Unit One

Writing Process

第一单元　写作过程

要点提示：写作是表达自我、阐述观点、描述事件、比较异同、辨析因果关系等的创造性过程。为求表达充分完整、论证合理有力、归纳分类得当、观点明确新颖，写作者应当遵循下列有益的步骤：善用"头脑风暴"激发灵感，汇集不同见解，丰富写作内涵；精心筛选信息，合理布局谋篇，拟定写作提纲；紧扣主题，酣畅淋漓地写就草稿；细致检查，反复修改，补充完善，成就理想的作品。

Introductory Remarks

Writing is an ongoing, recursive process from conception of the idea to final product presentation. It asserts that writing generally passes through some or all of the several clear steps including prewriting, drafting, and revising. These steps, however, don't provide a "one size fits all" solution for every writing situation. It is recursive and you can go back and forth between stages.

Writing is also a process of creation. It permits us to express our ideas, opinions, feelings, experiences, and even our frustrations; it offers us freedom that speech does not; it gives us more time to think over what we want to say, and it lets us put on paper what we may fear to say otherwise properly.

Warm-Up Exercise

Directions: Work out a list of the possible steps you are likely to follow when you write a composition.

Four Steps of Writing

Writing is a task that not two people accomplish in the same manner and magnitude because people differ in their attitudes toward the same subject or event. Besides, they may look at the same subject or event from completely different perspectives. However, there are some logical steps that every writer seems to follow in the creation of a paper. The process described below outlines those basic steps.

Step One：Brainstorming

Brainstorming is a process of enlisting your ideas and experiences about the assigned or selected subject. This step is probably the most important in writing because it is the one that gives you writing substance and provides you with the materials to develop your writing.

To have access to richer and more diversified materials before actually starting writing, it is advisable for you to work in teams as a source of generating ideas. Teams are often superior to individuals because they can accomplish more work, gather richer information, and offer more interpersonal communication dynamics. That said, teams, however, can waste time, accomplish little work, and create an environment in which interpersonal conflicts might rage out.

Many professionals, however, view teamwork as an efficient approach to collecting information in the process of writing. Teamwork usually generates new ideas by means of enabling members to be actively engaged with each other to express tentative and incomplete hypotheses without worrying about committing mistakes. Teamwork is informative for it helps students gain access to various sources of information instead of simply sitting back to listen to the instructor. And it is more demanding and challenging for students to be inquiring and thinking critically so that they can negotiate agreements out of arguable issues, work out solutions to problems they are facing, and contribute unique ideas as arguments to debates. Last but not least, teamwork provides students opportunities to benefit from the wisdom of their peers, and to tap into the ideas disclosed to make their writing more informative.

Mini-task: *Brainstorming*

Exercise One

Directions: Work out a list in small groups for "The Advantages and Disadvantages for College Students to Take Up a Part-time Job."

Exercise Two

Directions: Complete the two columns on "Traveling Alone."

Merits	Demerits

Step Two: Making an Outline—Organizing Your Ideas

An outline is a scheme of the organization of your paper. It indicates the main arguments for your thesis, supports the thesis, establishes the order and relationship of the main points, and clarifies the relationship between the major and minor points.

When you make an outline, you are organizing your ideas. You need to scan the brainstorming list you have worked out and decide what subject your ideas suggest. State this subject in a word or a phrase or a sentence, eliminate those ideas on the list that are not related to your stated subject, and organize your remaining ideas to support the subject.

Mini-task: *Case Analysis*

Directions: Analyze the following five outlines on "Traveling Alone" and pay attention to the differences among them.

Outline One

Paragraph One：Traveling alone is very profiting

Paragraph Two：Traveling alone is pretty dangerous

Paragraph Three：Conclusion

Outline Two

Paragraph One：Traveling alone has been gaining more and more popularity

Paragraph Two：Traveling alone is pretty challenging

Paragraph Three：More and more people, especially the youth, are traveling alone

Outline Three

Paragraph One：My first experience of traveling alone

Paragraph Two：Merits and demerits of traveling alone

Paragraph Three：An increasing number of people will travel alone in the future

Outline Four

Paragraph One：Traveling alone is a kind of adventure

Paragraph Two：Traveling alone is dangerous and complicated

Paragraph Three：Getting ready for traveling alone

Outline Five

Paragraph One：Necessity for traveling alone

Paragraph Two：How to travel alone

Paragraph Three：Rewards of traveling alone

Mini-task: *Outlining*

Directions：Make two outlines for "The Advantages and Disadvantages for College Students to Take Up a Part-time Job" with reference to the previous case analysis (Outlines for "Traveling Alone").

Outline One

Paragraph One：_____

Paragraph Two：_____

Paragraph Three：_____

Outline Two

Paragraph One：_____

Paragraph Two：_____

Paragraph Three: _____

Step Three: Drafting

The third step is to start the actual writing. When doing this, you need to scan your list of ideas and decide what these details suggest. You need also follow the outline you have worked out in Step Two. Although at times it is difficult to phrase out exactly what you mean, do not feel you are not successful if your ideas do not flow freely. It makes the writing easier if you start your writing by providing the outline with supporting points and feeding the paragraph with the brainstorming results. If you recall other ideas or details about the subject, also add them to your writing. Remember that information is always of the first importance in your writing; therefore, you are expected to make your writing as informative as possible.

Mini-task: *Drafting*

Directions: Write in around 150 words on "The Advantages and Disadvantages for College Students to Take Up a Part-time Job" according to the outline you have worked out.

Step Four: Revising

Your next step is to read your draft over, and to make changes to make sure it says what you wish to say. It is advisable for you to work in sharing groups to revise your writing. Sharing group engages group members most closely in sharing information, exchanging ideas, giving feedbacks, and providing comments so that you can improve your written work through the power of the collective mind of the group. The two critical points in sharing group work are listening and offering feedback. For listening, you must bear in mind that it involves more than just hearing. Hearing is a passive process, while listening is an active one. When listening, you are expected to give other group members your undivided attention, stay open-minded, avoid interrupting, and involve yourself in the communication. As for feedback, it is a must that it should be constructive. To achieve this objective, you should be aware of the need of feedback, the significance of both positive and negative feedback, and most importantly, the means of giving feedback. The following guidelines for compliments as well as complaints may help: Be descriptive. Relate objectively what you saw or what you heard. Give concrete examples; describe the behaviors and drop the labels;

don't exaggerate and try to be objective.

Mini-task: *Revising*

Directions：Revise your writing in sharing groups.

Homework

Task One：Readings on Writing Process

Directions：Read the following passages on writing process carefully and summarize the main points.

Passage One

Writing is a process that involves at least four steps：prewriting, drafting, revising, and editing. It is known as a recursive process. While you are revising, you might have to return to the prewriting step to develop and expand your ideas.

Prewriting

Prewriting is anything you do before you write a draft of your document. It includes thinking, taking notes, talking to others, brainstorming, outlining, and gathering information (e. g., interviewing people, researching in the library, assessing data).

Although prewriting is the first activity you engage in, generating ideas is an activity that occurs throughout the writing process.

Drafting

Drafting occurs when you put your ideas into sentences and paragraphs. Here you concentrate upon explaining and supporting your ideas fully. Here you also begin to connect your ideas. Regardless of how much thinking and planning you do, the process of putting your ideas in words changes them；often the very words you select evoke additional ideas or implications.

Don't pay too much attention to such things as spelling at this stage.

This draft tends to be **writer-centered**：it is you telling yourself what you know and think about the topic.

Revising

Revision is the key to effective writing. Here you think more deeply about your readers' needs and expectations. The paper becomes **reader-centered**. How much support will each idea need to convince your readers? Which terms should be defined for your particular readers? Is your organization effective? Do readers need to know X before they can understand Y?

At this stage you also refine your prose, making each sentence as concise and accurate as possible. Make connections between ideas explicit and clear.

Editing

Check for such things as grammar, mechanics, and spelling. The last thing you should do before printing your paper is to spell check it.

Don't edit your writing until the other steps in the writing process are complete.

Passage Two

The Elements of the Writing Process

While we can parse the writing process in various ways, it is perhaps simplest to see writing as a three-step process: pre-writing, writing, and re-writing.

Prewriting

Prewriting includes everything that a student does before beginning to draft a paper, such as generating ideas and organizing ideas.

Generating ideas. Experienced writing instructors offer students several strategies for generating ideas. Some of these strategies—like asking students to freewrite, or brainstorm, or write a discovery draft (a bit like free writing, but with more focus)—are more informal and can be used not only to come up with a topic but also to nudge a student out of a writing funk. Perhaps the best way of helping students to generate ideas is through good old-fashioned dialogue. Asking questions—in writing workshops—offers students a way of interrogating their ideas that will yield better papers.

Organizing ideas. Students have several strategies to choose from when organizing their ideas. Some students draft formal outlines and follow them faithfully as they write. Others make informal outlines that they revise as they draft. Some students find that sketching a paper works best for them: they start by writing down a possible thesis and then filling the page with related ideas, drawing arrows to establish possible connections, and using circles or stars or checkmarks to determine which ideas should be prioritized. Some students look for umbrella ideas and try to cluster related ideas beneath them. Still others write short paragraphs to initially summarize their thinking.

Writing

To begin to write is a difficult task. A writer sits at the keyboard, facing a blank screen, and must make the first decision that will begin the writing process. Most young writers suffer from one of three tendencies: 1) they are perfectionists and so keep writing the same first sentence again and again, trying to get it right; 2) they are terrified of making a decision and so continue to stare at the page as the clock ticks on; or 3) they see writing simply as the process of getting what's in their head onto the page. Once they've done a "brain dump" they think that the paper is finished. None of these writing strategies will yield a good paper in a timely fashion.

Students need to understand that writing tends to happen in two stages: first you write to express yourself, and then you write to make sense for your reader. More experienced writers have learned how to integrate the two stages by crafting their sentences and paragraphs as they write so that they express their ideas in ways that will engage their readers.

Writing is also understood by experienced writers as a recursive process. As writers draft, they discover new ideas and unexpected problems. At these junctures, they may have to return to earlier processes: they may brainstorm, re-sketch their ideas, and re-write their outlines. They will inevitably revise or refine their thesis. Some young writers will find this process discouraging.

Rewriting

Rewriting a paper is, for some students, even more difficult than writing it. Substantive revision requires that students re-envision their papers, trying to understand how readers are understanding or misunderstanding them.

Most students could benefit from a discussion of general reader expectations. Consider: Why do paragraphs require topic sentences? Because readers expect them. Where do they expect to find them? Generally at or near the beginning of a paragraph. When would you make an exception? When you're using a paragraph not to support a claim but to lead a reader to it; in this case, the topic sentence might come at the end of the paragraph. But regardless of where you put it, a topic sentence is needed in order to state, implicitly or explicitly, the paragraph's main idea. Why? Again, because readers expect it.

Readers' expectations can also help students revise their style. For instance, readers expect to find the main idea of a sentence in the main clause. If you've placed it elsewhere, the reader will have to work to figure out what you're trying to say.

Task Two: *Writing*

Directions: Write in around 120 words on "Formal Schooling Often Provides the Most Important Part of Learning." You are required to strictly follow the writing process we have discussed in this unit and hand in the sketch of brainstorming, outline, first draft, and revised version.

Unit Two

Wording Skills

第二单元　选词方法

要点提示：准确、简洁和多样化的用词是创造脍炙人口之作品的关键。在写作选词过程中，写作者应遵守语言习惯，避免中式英语；应仔细辨析近义词的差异，准确表达思想；应洞悉同一词语在中英文化背景下的不同内涵或不同词语在中英文化背景下的相同内涵，以免信息被误读；应尽量选择表意具体明确的词语；选择词语应尽量做到多样化，使读者将阅读作品变成一种享受，一个获取语言知识的源泉。

Introductory Remarks

What colors to painters and notes to musicians are what words to writers. Not merely do words have meaning, but also life, and hence they mark your personality, attitude, your understanding of your topic, and even, your understanding of life in general.

To represent life and experience exactly demands exact use of words, which, from a stylistic point of view, can be roughly classified into three categories: formal, informal, and colloquial. Knowledge of the levels of words matters, but the ability to use words accurately and properly makes a real writer.

Empirically, some words are general and others are concrete. Preferably, concrete words make your writing vivid, exact, clear, and hence more impressive and expressive. For instance, "good" is a general word, but "kind," "honest," "selfless," "compassionate," "soft-hearted," "gentle," "helpful," etc. , are more concrete and exact. To further illustrate the point, "laugh" is general, but "grin," "giggle," "chuckle," "smile," and "guffaw" designate a more specific kind of "laugh."

Even proper dictions are hardly always culturally proper. Cultural awareness and political correctness require that we bring to the surface our consciousness, our cultural awareness and political sense when we write (and speak). For instance, we cannot use the word nigger to refer to a black person, and nor can we use Chinaman for a Chinese, a Jap for a Japanese.

Warm-Up Exercise

Directions: Work out a list of possible reasons for the failure of using the right or appropriate words when you write.

Section One: Introduction to Chinglish and the Use of Idiomatic Expressions

Chinglish is any poor or broken English that is of Chinese origin. It is found both in written and spoken forms. Outstanding examples include "a cry of surprise," "I very much like you," and "how to say." These hardly exhaust a long list.

Generally, Chinglish is created out of deformed and grammatically erroneous usage of English, which shows the writer "thinks in Chinese while writing in English." Such examples include verbatim word-for-word translation, such as "three-good students," "good good study, day day up," and "I have something to do tomorrow." Be noted that Chinglish may also refer to the words and expressions created for the sake of humor. For example,

1. We two who and who?
2. You have seed, I will give you some color to see see.
3. I give you face, you don't want face.
4. Know is know, noknow is noknow.
5. People mountain, people sea.

Mini-task

Directions: Discuss in small groups each pair of expressions given below. You are required to compare and contrast the two expressions in each pair and analyze the reasons for using the respective Chinglish expressions.

1. Dad always likes losing his temper.
   Dad is apt to lose his temper.
2. He is always red-eyed of other people's achievements.
   He is always green-eyed of other people's achievements.
3. You should drink more white boiled water in summer.
   You should drink more plain boiled water in summer.
4. I don't dance well too.
   I am not a very good dancer either.
5. What time is it now?
   What time is it, please?
6. Would you like to join our party on Friday?
   Would you like to come to our party on Friday night?
7. His body is healthy.
   He is in good health.
8. We got off the car.
   We got out of the car.
9. The speed of the car is fast.
   The car is speeding. /The car is going too fast.
10. If you have trouble, ask for the policeman.
    In cases of trouble, ask for the police.
11. Don't forget to take your thing.
    Don't forget your personal belongings.

Section Two: Introduction to the Difference Between Concrete Words and General Words

Concrete words refer to particular things, while general terms are concerned with classes or groups of things. Usually, general words do not appeal imaginatively to the reader's senses, or evoke hazy pictures, whereas concrete words generate more vivid pictures. Although both general and concrete words are necessary for effective communication, it is suggested that you use specific and concrete words to make your writing effective. After you read the given pairs of examples, you might get a better understanding of the difference between concrete and general words.

1. She is a junior student.

   She is a third-year student.

2. John is a good teacher.

   John is a responsible teacher.

3. There are five people in the room.

   There are five girl students in the classroom.

4. Helen is an educator.

   Helen is a university instructor.

5. Bill is a scientist.

   Bill is a biologist.

Mini-task

Directions: Circle the most concrete word in each numbered group below. Consult your seatmates for the meaning of unfamiliar terms.

1. meat   chicken   fried chicken

2. dessert   lemon icebox pie   pie

3. blue jeans   clothes   pants

4. North America   New Jersey   United States

5. pen   ball point   writing instrument

6. rose   plant   flower

7. mammal   mouse   animal

8. poultry   livestock   ducks

9. silverware   salad fork   fork

10. transportation automobile   Buick

Section Three: Introduction to Words with Subtle Difference

What challenges Chinese students most when writing in English appears to be making proper choice of words with subtle difference, such as the difference of the following paired sentences:

1. He is the winner.

   He is on the win.

2. We are secure.

   We are safe.

3. She is narrow-minded.

   She is petty.

4. Jerry found a good job at last.

   Jerry landed a satisfactory job.

5. The victim is in the hospital.

   The victim is hospitalized.

Mini-task

Directions: Discuss in small groups the subtle difference in the paired sentences below.

1. You will never meet this chance again in your life.

   This is a once-in-a-life-time chance.

2. Jobless rate hit 5.7% in the third quarter.

   Jobless rate reached 5.7% in the third quarter.

3. It is estimated that more jobs will be cut in the quarter ahead.

   It is estimated that more jobs will be reduced in the next season.

4. Students can't afford to miss job fairs.

   Students can't afford to miss job ads.

5. The minimum wage differs from state to state in the United States.

   The lowest wage differs from state to state in the United States.

6. I'm calling to see if help is needed at your restaurant.

   I'm calling to see whether I can get a job at your restaurant.

7. Can you give me a cigarette?

   Can you spare me a cigarette?

8. Dancers wanted. For day shift.

   Dancers wanted. For day work.

9. 30 days money back guarantee.

   We will return you the money within 30 days.

10. Big money, small hour.

    You will earn a lot of money in a very short time.

11. The criminal is on the run.

The criminal is running.

12. A standby witnessed the crime.

A standby saw the crime.

Examples

1. advance / advanced

When you hear about something in advance, you get notice or information earlier than other people. "Advanced" means "complex, sophisticated" and doesn't necessarily have anything to do with the revealing of secrets.

2. advice / advise

"Advice" is a noun, "advise" a verb. When Ann Landers advises people, she gives them advice.

3. affect/effect

"Affect" is usually a verb meaning "to influence". "Effect" is usually a noun meaning "result". The drug did not affect the disease, and it had several adverse side effects. "Effect" can also be a verb meaning "to bring about". Only the president can effect such a dramatic change.

4. appraise / apprise

When you estimate the value of something, you appraise it. When you inform people of a situation, you apprise them of it.

5. aspect / respect

When used to refer to different elements of or perspectives on something or an idea, these words are closely related, but not interchangeable. It is "in all respects," not "in all aspects." Similarly, one can say "in some respects" but not "in some aspects." One says "in this respect," not "in this aspect." One looks at all "aspects" of an issue, not at all "respects."

6. assure / ensure / insure

To "assure" a person of something is to make him or her confident of it. According to Associated Press Style, to "ensure" that something happens is to make certain that it does, and to "insure" is to issue an insurance policy. Other authorities, however, consider "ensure" and "insure" interchangeable. To please conservatives, it is necessary to make the distinction. However, it is worth noting that in older usage these spellings were not clearly distinguished.

European life assurance companies take the position that all policy-holders are mortal and someone will definitely collect, thus "assuring" heirs of some income. American companies tend to go with "insurance" for coverage of life as well as of fire, theft, house, auto, etc.

7. attribute / contribute

When trying to give credit to someone, you "attribute" your success to their help, not "contribute". (Of course, a politician may attribute his success to those who contribute to his campaign fund, but probably only in private.)

8. backward / backwards

As an adverb, either word will do: "put the shirt on backward" or "put the shirt on backwards." However, as an adjective, only "backward" will do: "a backward glance." When in doubt, use "backward."

9. belief / believe

If you have it, it is a "belief"; if you do it, you "believe". People can't have religious "believes"; they have religious "beliefs".

10. biweekly / semiweekly

Technically, a biweekly meeting occurs every two weeks and a semiweekly one occurs twice a week, but so few people get this straight that your club is liable to disintegrate unless you avoid these words in the newsletter and stick with "every other week" or "twice weekly." The same is true of "bimonthly" and "semimonthly," though "biennial" and "semi-annual" are less often confused with each other.

Mini-task

Directions: Discuss in small groups the differences in meaning and usage of the paired words.

1. continuous / continual
2. criteria / criterion
3. democrat / democratic
4. vary / differ
5. dilemma / difficulty
6. ecology / environment
7. economical / economic
8. emigrate / immigrate
9. eminent / imminent
10. enquire / inquire

11. fearful / fearsome
12. footnotes / endnotes
13. formally / formerly
14. Internet / intranet
15. later / latter

Section Four: Appropriate Use of Words in a Given Cultural Context

Examples

1. Every dog has its day.
   Every person has a happy day.
2. He is strong as horse.
   He is strong as ox.
3. Drink like a fish.
   Drink like a hippo.
4. The Four Tigers of Asia.
   The Four Dragons of Asia.
5. He is a chicken.
   He is a mouse.

Mini-task

Directions: Work out a list of words that are not used appropriately in your writings in a given cultural context.

Homework

Task One

Directions: Tell the difference between the two given words in each pair.
1. lay / lie
2. myths / legends

3. like / as if

4. luxuriant / luxurious

5. majority is / majority are

6. online / on line

7. oral / verbal

8. exaggerated / over-exaggerated

9. oversee / overlook

10. passed / past

11. persecute / prosecute

12. personal / personnel

13. phenomena / phenomenon

14. premise / premises

15. principal / principle

16. proved / proven

17. purposely / purposefully

18. rational / rationale

19. reason / because

20. recent / resent

21. regrettabe / regrettful

22. ironic / sarcastic

23. sole / soul

24. sometime / some time

25. specially / especially

26. states / countries

27. taken back / taken aback

28. today's modern society / today

29. very unique / unique

30. wander / wonder

Task Two

Directions: Identify the errors in the following expressions, and try to correct them.

1. Sorry, I forgot my textbook at home.

2. I feel very painful in my right hand.

3. He looked at her and felt surprised.

4. I have read your novels but I didn't think you could be so young.

5. Dad always likes losing his temper.

6. He is always red-eyed of other people's achievements.

7. You should drink more white boiled water in summer.

8. Chinese is our mother language.

9. My grandpa is running for seventy-five.

10. The price is very suitable for me.

11. Her red face made me see through her mind.

12. The sight of these pictures made me remember my own childhood.

13. Don't pay attention to her.

14. I get a lot of knowledge in the university.

15. Samuel is reading a book.

16. She was so jealous that she became desperate.

Task Three: Reading

Directions: Read the given passages below carefully and pay close attention to the underlined words and expressions.

Passage One（A Report on Shooting）

A 17-year-old girl was gun down this morning at 6 when she was driving home together with two guys. Another car approached them and fired the girl at her head. She died on the way to the hospital. The murder is not yet identified and the case is still under investigation.

Passage Two（Commercial）

Are you looking for an overnight getaway for you and your special someone? It's right here in Chicago. Make it now! Make it tomorrow! Make it right here in Chicago!

Passage Three（A Wanted Ad）

We offer flexible schedule, and opportunity for growth. Weekly paycheck. Paid vacations. Friendly working environment. Salary plus bonus, tuition reimbursement, employee stock purchase plan, leading edge sales training program, excellent benefits package including medical and dental insurance plans. You/the candidates offer: interpersonal skills; energetic and dependable professionalism, independence and self-motivation plus strong competitive sales drive and a commitment to excel, leadership skills, a strong work ethic, previous experience is a plus; knowledge of computers and software and good written and verbal skills.

Passage Four (**Job Cut**)

Everyday, we get more and more announcements of job cuts. In last 3 months over 800,000 jobs were cut. It's estimated that more jobs will be cut in the quarter ahead. No improvement can be expected until the first quarter next year.

Passage Five (**Job Fairs**)

Anderson, assistant director of career management at UIC, said, "Students can't afford to miss job fairs." On-campus job fairs are where connections are made; company representatives and students follow up on job fair connections, and create career opportunities for the future.

Passage Six (**Job Seeking**)

Landing a good job means managing to get a good job. Riyal plans to pursue a master's degree in business administration if he doesn't land a good job after graduation. Recession or not, Anderson said, perseverance is key to landing a good job. Students must follow up when making contacts with companies, after handing out resumes and after the interview process.

Passage Seven (**Communication Skills**)

Regardless of whom you are listening to or what the topic is, keep your emotions in check, listen objectively, and think of it as a win-win situation: The speaker wins by convincing you of the merits of his or her position, and you win by gaining new information and insights that will help you perform your duties more effectively.

Passage Eight (**Baggage Claim**)

It's time to get your bags. Follow signs to the baggage claim. TV monitors will tell you exactly where your baggage will arrive. After you get your baggage, go through customs. If you have something to declare, go through the red exit. If not, go through the green one. We hope you enjoy your stay in China. Have a nice day.

Task Four: *Rewriting*

Directions: Read the following two paragraphs carefully and underline the mistakes in word choice and then rewrite the two paragraphs in appropriate words and expressions.

Paragraph One

Miss Wang is a small girl. She distinguishes herself with her beauty. Her beauty is without comparison. She has two big eyes. Her eyes are wide open and full of water and her hair floats down like a waterfall. She likes tidy and her clothes are all new. She impresses me deeply and gives me a very deep mark. what I love the girl.

Paragraph Two

As a real friend, when you are doing fine, he may be isn't about you. But when it is rain, he will take a umbrella for you. A false friend is different. when he needs you, he comes to you. When you go to trouble, he goes away. He is a man with a little heart.

Unit Three

Figures of Speech

第三单元　修　辞　格

要点提示：修辞是一种艺术，它是强化语言信息、提升语言感染力和增强语言表达效果的特殊语言手段，它使我们说话、写文章得体、优美和有效。人们在语言实践中自觉或不自觉地运用修辞。在写作、交际过程中，我们可从语音、词法和句法等层面适当使用一些修辞格来遣词造句、谋篇布局，使语言表达生动、活泼，使语言交际准确有效。

Introductory Remarks

Language is the primary means of human communication. Effective communication is realized through the use of precise and appropriate words and sentences. We are said to be speaking or writing figuratively when we use words in non-literal senses to lend force to an idea, to heighten effectiveness of expression, or to create mode or atmosphere. For example, it is more vivid and colorful to say that stars "twinkle like diamonds" in the sky, than to say simply that they "shine brightly" in the sky.

Whether speaking or writing, we have to get ourselves across effectively, i. e. to be expressive, persuasive, and impressive. Figurative language when used properly brings freshness, vigor and resonance to our speech and writing. It helps its audience understand connections better through comparison.

Warm-Up Exercise

Directions：Work out some figures of speech in small groups and tell their functions in speaking or writing.

Introduction to Figures of Speech

According to *Longman Modern English Dictionary*, a figure of speech is "an unusual, esp. metaphorical mode of expression, used for effect in speech and writing, and to clarify or deepen meaning by suggesting similitudes which provoke thought." J. C. Richards defines it as "a word or phrase which is used for special effect, and which does not have its usual or literal meaning." Figures of speech are devices to be employed for special effect in speech or writing. They arise when the mind associates one thing with another because they are similar or dissimilar in some respects, or related in common experience for the sake of emphasis. In this book, we discuss figures of speech at phonetic, lexical and syntactical levels.

1. Alliteration

Alliteration is a figure of speech in which the same consonant sound or sound group is repeated at intervals in the initial position of words. It is also called "head rhyme" or "front rhyme." It is used to achieve rhythmic effect, and catch readers' or listeners' attention. For example：

(1) Penny wise, pound foolish.

(2) Willful waste makes woeful want.

(3) Without wisdom, wealth is worthless.

(4) Our hopes, our hearts, our hands are with those on every continent who are building democracy and freedom.　　　　(B. Clinton, "Inaugural Address")

(5) We shape our own destiny with conviction, compassion, and clear and common purpose.　　　　(B. Obama, "Weekly Address, November 25th, 2010")

(6) I slip, I slide, I gloom, I glance,
Among my skimming swallows；

(A. Tennyson, "The Brook")

(7) The fair breeze blew, the white foam flew,

The furrow followed free;

We were the first that ever burst,

Into that silent sea.

(S. T. Coleridge, *The Rime of the Ancient Mariner*)

2. Rhyme

Rhyme refers to the sameness or similarity in the sound of word endings, employed usually at the end of lines in verse. It is regarded as verbal music made through identity of sound in the final syllables of words. For example:

(1) Haste makes waste.

(2) Man proposes, God disposes.

(3) Little strokes fell great oaks.

(4) Genius is two percent inspiration and ninety-eight percent perspiration.

(5) His great gaunt figure filled the cabin door,

And had he fallen inward on the floor,

He must have measured to the further wall.

(R. Frost, "The Figure in the Doorway")

(6) Most souls, tis true, but peep out once an age,

Dull sullen pris'ners in the body's cage.

(A. Pope, "Elegy to the Memory of an Unfortunate Lady")

3. Simile

A simile is a figure of speech in which an explicit comparison between two distinctly different things is indicated by the word "as" or "like," etc. For example:

(1) My roommates stood there as motionless as statues.

(2) Living without an aim is like sailing without a compass.

(3) Ambition is to life just what steam is to the locomotive.

(4) He speaks as there were a frog in his throat.

(5) I wandered lonely as a cloud.

(6) My heart is like a singing bird.

(7) Beauty is as summer fruits, which are easy to corrupt and cannot last.

(8) He was a beautiful horse that looked as though he had come out of a painting by Velasquez.

4. Metaphor

Metaphor is a figure of speech in which there is an implicit comparison between two or more unlike elements. "Language is vitally metaphorical." Appropriate use of metaphor can help us achieve good rhetorical effect. As Aristotle points out, "It is metaphor above all else that gives clearness, charm and distinction to the style." For example:

(1) Life is a journey.

(2) Jim was a fox.

(3) She is the apple of his eye.

(4) The news is a dagger to his heart.

(5) Habit is a cable; every day we weave a thread and soon we cannot break it.

(6) In short, winter is a tomb, spring is a lie, and summer is a pernicious mirage.

(7) All the world's a stage,

And all the men and women merely players;

They have their exits and their entrances,

And one man in his time plays many parts,

His acts being seven ages...

(W. Shakespeare, *As You Like It*)

5. Metonymy

Metonymy is a figure of speech in which the name of one thing is substituted for that of another with which it is closely associated. In other words, it involves a "change of name," the substituted name suggesting the thing meant. Metonymy is a very useful and effective rhetorical device, for it compresses much into a single word or short noun phrase. For example:

(1) He drank a cup.

(2) She set a good table.

(3) He is fond of the bottle.

(4) Have you read Jack London?

(5) Gray hair should be respected.

(6) The pen is mightier than the sword.

(7) He has been appointed to the bench.

(8) Some say the world will end in fire, some say in ice.

6. Synecdoche

Synecdoche is a figure of speech in which an expression denoting a part is used to refer to a whole, or vice versa. Synecdoche contributes to the vitality and variety of the writing. Look at the following examples:

(1) The kettle is boiling.

(2) Great minds think alike.

(3) He smokes two packs per day.

(4) The poor creature could no longer endure her sufferings.

(5) The farms were short of hands during the harvest season.

(6) It was reported that Britain beat New Zealand in the football match yesterday.

(7) He paid the workers $5 per head.

7. Personification

Personification is a figure of speech in which a thing or an idea is treated as if it were human or had human qualities. For example:

(1) Fear gripped his heart.

(2) This time fate was smiling to him.

(3) His words sent a quiver through my body.

(4) Dusk found the boy wandering down the street.

(5) The thick carpet killed the sound of my footsteps.

(6) The morning sun greeted us as we came out on deck.

(7) I have been the sport and toy of debasing circumstances. Ignominy, Want, Despair, and Madness, have collectively or separately, been the attendants of my career.

(C. Dickens, David Copperfield)

(8) In November, a cold, unseen stranger, whom the doctors called Pneumonia, stalked about the colony, touching one here and there with his icy fingers. Over the east side the ravager strode boldly, smiting his victims by scores.

(O. Henry, "The Last Leaf")

8. Hyperbole

Hyperbole, also called overstatement, is the deliberate use of exaggeration for emphasis. It is often used to express one's feelings by remarkable imagination and literary extravagance, for the effect of strong impression, humor, sarcasm, irony, etc. For example:

(1) I'm the luckiest man in the world.

(2) Belinda smiled, and all the world was gay.

(3) The noise was big enough to wake the dead.

(4) One father is more than a hundred schoolmasters.

(5) She was beautiful—her beauty made the bright world dim...

(6) Polly, I love you. You are the whole world to me, and the moon and the stars and

the constellations of outer space.

(7) I loved Ophelia: forty thousand brothers could not, with all their quantity of love, make up my sum.

(W. Shakespeare, *Hamlet*)

9. Oxymoron

Oxymoron is a figure of speech in which apparently contrasting, contradictory or incongruous words are used to achieve a special or epigrammatic effect. It is employed to make emphasis, to produce humor or sharp contrast. It was widely used in poetry, especially in the 16th and 17th centuries. Below are some examples:

(1) My only love sprung from my only hate.

(2) The coach had to be cruel to be kind to his trainees.

(3) I like a smuggler. He was the only honest thief.

(4) No light, but rather darkness visible.

(5) The verdict was guilty. I was fined 100 dollars and costs. Dudley Field Malone called my conviction a "victorious defeat."

(6) Beautiful tyrant! fiend angelical!
    Dove feather's raven! wolfish-ravening lamb!
    Despised substance of divinest show!
    Just opposite to what thou justly seem'st,
    A damn saint, an honorable villain!

(W. Shakespeare, *Romeo and Juliet*)

10. Euphemism

Euphemism is substitution of an agreeable or inoffensive expression for one that may offend or suggest something unpleasant. Fowler calls it "slurring over badness by giving it a good name." For example:

(1) The girl is hard of hearing.

(2) The boy is a bit slow for his age.

(3) It is five years since he passed away.

(4) I'm afraid he has distorted the fact.

(5) He was short of money, so he had to buy a pre-owned car.

(6) In private I should merely call him a liar. In the press you should use the words: "Reckless disregard for truth" and in parliament—that you regret he "should have been so misinformed."

(J. Galsworthy, *Silver Spoon*)

11. Parallelism

Parallelism refers to the parallel presentation of two or more than two similar or relevant ideas in similar structural forms. It helps clarify the relationship between a writer's parallel ideas, or between parallel parts of a single idea, by expressing relevant ideas and identical tone in the same or similar grammatical structure. It often results in linguistic brevity, structural balance and pleasant rhythm. It can be formed of a series of words, phrases, clauses, and sentences. For example:

(1) He doesn't ride, nor shoot, nor fish, nor swim.

(2) Lumber, corn, tobacco, wheat, and furs moved downstream to the delta country.

(3) An Englishman thinks seated; a Frenchman, standing; an American, pacing; an Irishman, afterward.

(4) Women were running out to the line of march, crying and laughing and kissing the men goodbye.

(J. Killens, "God Bless America")

(5) We can gain knowledge by reading, by reflection, by observation or by practice.

(6) Let every nation know, whether it wishes us well or ill, that we shall pay any price, bear any burden, meet any hardship, support any friend, oppose any foe to assure the survival and the success of liberty.

(7) Reading makes a full man, conference a ready man, and writing an exact man.

(8) There is no reason for us to be enemies. Neither of us seeks the territory of the other; neither of us seeks domination over the other; neither of us seeks to stretch out our hands and rule the world.

(A Toast by President Richard Nixon on His First Visit to China in 1972)

(9) And so, my fellow Americans, ask not what your country can do for you: Ask what you can do for your country.

(J. F. Kennedy, "Inaugural Address")

12. Antithesis

Antithesis is the placing of opposed ideas or characteristics in direct contrast with each other. It is often balanced in structure, and contrastive in meaning. If well used, it can result in linguistic brevity and rhythmic harmony. For example:

(1) Speech is silver; silence is gold.

(2) We find ourselves rich in goods, but ragged in spirit, reaching with magnificent precision for the moon, but falling into raucous discord on earth.

(R. Nixon)

(3) I had walked into that reading room a happy healthy man. I crawled out a decrepit wreck.

(J. K. Jerome, "The Three Men in a Boat")

(4) It was the best of times, it was the worst of times; it was the age of wisdom, it was the age of foolishness; it was the epoch of belief, it was the epoch of incredulity; it was the season of light, it was the season of darkness; it was the spring of hope, it was the winter of despair; we had everything before us, we had nothing before us; we were all going direct to Heaven, we were all going direct the other way.

(C. Dickens, *A Tale of Two Cities*)

13. Repetition

Repetition is the use of the same words close together in sentences or paragraphs. It is a rhetorical device which is employed to emphasize a statement or to express a strong emotion. For example:

(1) Light come, light go.

(2) Diamond cuts diamond.

(3) If slavery is not wrong, nothing is wrong.

(4) We must all hang together, or we shall all hang separately.

(5) Money makes him get everything; money makes him lose everything.

(6) There is no absolute good; there is nothing absolutely right. All things flow and change, and even change is not absolute.

(D. H. Lawrence, "Why the Novel Matters")

(7) And then suddenly the machines pushed them out and they swarmed on the highways. The movement changed them; the highways, the camps along the road, the fear of hunger and the hunger itself, changed them. The children without dinner changed them, the endless moving changed them. They were migrants. And the hostility changed them, welded them, united them...

(J. Steinbeck, *The Grapes of Wrath*)

14. Loose sentence

From a rhetorical point of view, sentences are loose and periodic. A loose sentence puts the main idea before all supplementary information. Compared with periodic sentences, loose sentences are easier, simpler, more natural and direct. For example:

(1) She decided to study English though she was interested in music.

(2) The Smiths must have gone away for the holidays, for we have not seen them for

about two weeks.

(3) Ursula and Gudrun Brangwen sat one morning in the window-bay of their father's house in Beldover, working and talking. Ursula was stitching a piece of brightly-colored embroidery, and Gudrun was drawing upon a board which she held on her knee. They were mostly silent, talking as their thoughts strayed through their minds.

(D. H. Lawrence, *Women in Love*)

15. Periodic sentence

In contrast to the loose sentence, a periodic sentence has its main idea at or near the end of the sentence. The reader does not know what is mainly about until he finishes reading it. Periodic sentences are more complex, emphatic, formal or literary. For example:

(1) As we paddled southwest past the candle factory, the rain beat against us.

(2) Although she was interested in music, she finally decided to study English.

(3) It is a truth universally acknowledged, that a single man in possession of a good fortune must be in want of a wife.

(J. Austen)

(4) To believe your own thought, to believe that what is true for you in your private heart is true for all men—that is genius.

(R. W. Emerson)

(5) The great question that has never been answered, and which I have not yet been able to answer despite my thirty years of research into the feminine soul, is this, "what does a woman want?"

(S. Freud)

16. Climax

Climax refers to the rising arrangement of a series of ideas which go from the least important to the most important with steady strengthening of emotion and tone, so that the greatest strength or chief point of interest is at the end. It is often used by speakers and writers in their persuasive speech or writing, and it is extremely effective in stirring up feelings and emotions. Here are some examples:

(1) I came, I saw, I conquered.

(2) Some books are to be tasted, others to be swallowed, and some to be chewed and digested.

(F. Bacon, "Of Studies")

(3) But in a large sense we cannot dedicate, we cannot consecrate, we cannot hallow

this ground.

(4) For some men gambling leads to penury, penury to petty theft, petty theft to robbery, robbery to armed violence, and armed violence to murder.

(A. Lincoln)

(5) It is an outrage to bind a Roman citizen; to scourge him is a crime; to put him to death is almost parricide.

(M. T. Cicero)

(6) He who loses wealth loses much; he who loses a friend loses more; but he who loses courage loses all.

(7) To acquire wealth is difficult, to preserve it more difficult, but to spend it wisely most difficult.

17. Anticlimax

Anticlimax is the opposite of climax and is a rhetorical device that involves one's thoughts in a descending order of significance or intensity, from strong to weak. "It is a sentence in which the last part expresses something lower than the first." Hence it is called "the art of sinking" by Pope. It is usually employed for jocular and humorous effect. Take the following for example:

(1) For God, for America, and for Yale.

(2) He lost his empire, his family and his fountain pen.

(3) The duties of a soldier are to protect his country and peel potatoes.

(4) The explosion completely destroyed a church, two houses, and a flowerpot.

(5) There is nothing more exhilarating to the nature-lover than an early morning walk in the foot hill of the Himalayas. It lifts his spirit above material concerns and inspires in him noble thought. It also makes him hungry.

18. Rhetorical question

Rhetorical question is a device used for emphasis or transition. Basically it is not expecting an answer. It is used primarily for stylistic effect, and is a very common rhetorical device in public speaking. For example:

(1) The crowd stands silent and erect, but, even in that piecing cold, heads are bared...there are no speeches, for who can speak at such a moment?

(2) Fellow citizens, pardon me, allow me to ask, why am I called upon to speak here today? What have I, or those I represent, to do with your national independence? Are the great principles of political freedom and natural justice, embodied in that Declaration of Independence, extended to us?

Mini-task

Directions: Identify the figures of speech in the following sentences.

1. Spring, sweet spring is the year's pleasant king.
2. Time and tide wait for no man.
3. She has to earn her daily bread by doing odd jobs.
4. He has been called to the bar.
5. The wind whistled through the tree.
6. An atmosphere of dangerous calmness could be felt throughout the mining region.
7. Your jokes really kill me.
8. O, Wind, if winter comes, can spring be far behind? (P. B. Shelly)
9. Golf does queer things to the players. The average man will show greater distress more openly over the loss of a golf ball than over the loss of his business, his home or a close relation.
10. Education is not the filling of a pail, but the lighting of a fire. (W. Yeats)
11. Marriage is like a beleaguered fortress: those who are without want to get in, and those within want to get out. (P. M. Quitard)
12. Gorki himself was a man of such great courage, of such deep simplicity and of such intense honesty.
13. He took a standard train compartment to go back home for weekends.
14. Would you please please please please please please please please stop talking? (E. Hemingway)
15. The coward man does it with a kiss, the brave man with a sword. (O. Wilde)
16. Lincoln recognized worth in the common people; he loved the common people; he fought for the common people; and he died for the common people.
17. Badly frightened by the explosion, the boy rushed out of the laboratory.
18. I saw the naked simplicities of the complicated civilization in which I lived. (J. London)
19. Reading is to the mind what exercise is to the body. (R. Steel)
20. If not always in a hot mood to smash, the sea is always stealthily ready for a drowning. (J. Conrad)

Homework

Directions：Read the following two passages, and identity figures of speech that you find the most effective.

Of Studies

Francis Bacon

Studies serve for delight, for ornament, and for ability. Their chief use for delight, is in privateness and retiring; for ornament, is in discourse; and for ability, is in the judgment and disposition of business. For expert man can execute, and perhaps judge of particulars, one by one; but the general counsels, and the plots and marshalling of affairs, come best from those that are learned.

To spend too much time in studies is sloth; to use them too much for ornament, is affectation; to make judgment wholly by their rules, is the humor of a scholar. They perfect nature, and are perfected by experience; for natural abilities are like natural plants, that need pruning by study; and studies themselves do give forth directions too much at large, except they be bounded in by experience.

Crafty men condemn studies; simple men admire them; and wise men use them: for they teach not their own use; but that is a wisdom without them, and above them, won by observation. Read not to contradict and confute; nor to believe and take for granted; nor to find talk and discourse; but to weigh and consider.

Some books are to be tasted, others to be swallowed, and some few to be chewed and digested: that is, some books are to be read only in parts; others to be read, but not curiously; and some few to be read wholly, and with diligence and attention. Some books also may be read by deputy, and extracts made of them by others; but that would be only in the less important arguments, and the meaner sort of books; else distilled books are, like common distilled waters, flashy things.

Reading maketh a full man; conference a ready man; and writing an exact man. And therefore, if a man write little, he had need have a great memory; if he confer little, he had need have a present wit; and if he read little, he had need have much cunning, to seem to know that he doth not. Histories make men wise; poets witty; the mathematics subtle; natural philosophy deep; moral grave; logic and rhetoric able to contend. *Abeunt studia in* mores.

Nay, there is no stond or impediment in the wit, but may be wrought out by fit studies: like as diseases of the body may have appropriate exercises. Bowling is good for the stone and reins; shooting for the lungs and breast; gentle walking for the stomach; riding for the head; and the like.

So if a man's wit be wandering, let him study the mathematics; for in demonstrations, if his wit be called away never so little, he must begin again. If his wit be not apt to distinguish or find differences, let him study the schoolmen; for they are *cymini sectores*. If he be not apt to beat over matters, and to call up one thing to prove and illustrate another, let him study the lawyers' cases. So every defect of the mind may have a special receipt.

Barack Obama's Victory Speech

If there is anyone out there who still doubts that America is a place where all things are possible; who still wonders if the dream of our founders is alive in our time; who still questions the power of our democracy, tonight is your answer.

It's the answer told by lines that stretched around schools and churches in numbers this nation has never seen; by people who waited three hours and four hours, many for the very first time in their lives, because they believed that this time must be different; that their voice could be that difference.

It's the answer spoken by young and old, rich and poor, Democrat and Republican, black, white, Latino, Asian, Native American, gay, straight, disabled and not disabled— Americans who sent a message to the world that we have never been a collection of Red States and Blue States: We are, and always will be, the United States of America.

It's the answer that led those who have been told for so long by so many to be cynical, and fearful, and doubtful of what we can achieve to put their hands on the arc of history and bend it once more toward the hope of a better day.

...

The road ahead will be long. Our climb will be steep. We may not get there in one year or even one term, but America—I have never been more hopeful than I am tonight that we will get there. I promise you—we as a people will get there.

There will be setbacks and false starts. There are many who won't agree with every decision or policy I make as President, and we know that government can't solve every problem. But I will always be honest with you about the challenges we face. I will listen to you, especially when we disagree. And above all, I will ask you to join in the work of remaking this nation the only way it's been done in America for two-hundred and twenty-one years—block by block, brick by brick, calloused hand by calloused hand.

What began twenty-one months ago in the depths of winter must not end on this autumn night. This victory alone is not the change we seek—it is only the chance for us to make that change. And that cannot happen if we go back to the way things were. It cannot happen without you.

So let us summon a new spirit of patriotism; of service and responsibility where each of us resolves to pitch in and work harder and look after not only ourselves, but each other. Let us remember that if this financial crisis taught us anything, it's that we cannot have a thriving Wall Street while Main Street suffers—in this country, we rise or fall as one nation; as one people.

Let us resist the temptation to fall back on the same partisanship and pettiness and immaturity that has poisoned our politics for so long. Let us remember that it was a man from this state who first carried the banner of the Republican Party to the White House—a party founded on the values of self-reliance, individual liberty, and national unity. Those are values we all share, and while the Democratic Party has won a great victory tonight, we do so with a measure of humility and determination to heal the divides that have held back our progress. As Lincoln said to a nation far more divided than ours, "We are not enemies, but friends though passion may have strained it must not break our bonds of affection." And to those Americans whose support I have yet to earn—I may not have won your vote, but I hear your voices, I need your help, and I will be your President too.

And to all those watching tonight from beyond our shores, from parliaments and palaces to those who are huddled around radios in the forgotten corners of our world—our stories are singular, but our destiny is shared, and a new dawn of American leadership is at hand. To those who would tear this world down—we will defeat you. To those who seek peace and security—we support you. And to all those who have wondered if America's beacon still burns as bright—tonight we proved once more that the true strength of our nation comes not from the might of our arms or the scale of our wealth, but from the enduring power of our ideals: democracy, liberty, opportunity, and unyielding hope.

For that is the true genius of America—that America can change. Our union can be perfected. And what we have already achieved gives us hope for what we can and must achieve tomorrow.

This election had many firsts and many stories that will be told for generations. But one that's on my mind tonight is about a woman who cast her ballot in Atlanta. She's a lot like the millions of others who stood in line to make their voice heard in this election except for one thing—Ann Nixon Cooper is 106 years old.

She was born just a generation past slavery; a time when there were no cars on the road or planes in the sky; when someone like her couldn't vote for two reasons—because she was a woman and because of the color of her skin.

And tonight, I think about all that she's seen throughout her century in America—the heartache and the hope; the struggle and the progress; the times we were told that we can't, and the people who pressed on with that American creed. Yes we can.

At a time when women's voices were silenced and their hopes dismissed, she lived to see them stand up and speak out and reach for the ballot. Yes we can.

When there was despair in the dust bowl and depression across the land, she saw a nation conquer fear itself with a New Deal, new jobs and a new sense of common purpose. Yes we can.

When the bombs fell on our harbor and tyranny threatened the world, she was there to witness a generation rise to greatness and a democracy was saved. Yes we can.

She was there for the buses in Montgomery, the hoses in Birmingham, a bridge in Selma, and a preacher from Atlanta who told a people that "We Shall Overcome." Yes we can.

A man touched down on the moon, a wall came down in Berlin, a world was connected by our own science and imagination. And this year, in this election, she touched her finger to a screen, and cast her vote, because after 106 years in America, through the best of times and the darkest of hours, she knows how America can change. Yes we can.

America, we have come so far. We have seen so much. But there is so much more to do. So tonight, let us ask ourselves—if our children should live to see the next century; if my daughters should be so lucky to live as long as Ann Nixon Cooper, what change will they see? What progress will we have made?

This is our chance to answer that call. This is our moment. This is our time—to put our people back to work and open doors of opportunity for our kids; to restore prosperity and promote the cause of peace; to reclaim the American Dream and reaffirm that fundamental truth—that out of many, we are one; that while we breathe, we hope, and where we are met with cynicism, and doubt, and those who tell us that we can't, we will respond with that timeless creed that sums up the spirit of a people.

Yes We Can. Thank you, God bless you, and may God Bless the United States of America.

Unit Four
Topic Sentence Paragraph

第四单元 主题句段落

要点提示：主题句是对段落主旨的高度概括，因而有助于作者把握段落方向，避免"下笔千言，离题万里"；有利于读者快捷领悟作者意图，提高阅读效率。主题句的位置灵活，可置于段首、段中、段尾，亦可同时置于段首和段尾，以实现强调主旨之目的。但写好主题句并非易事：过于宽泛，则段落难以专注特定主旨；过于具体，则段落无法进一步推展。如何做到宽窄得当、中心思想明确，是主题句段落写作的难点和重点。

Introductory Remarks

Sentences vary: there are a good number of types of sentences such as declarative, interrogative, imperative, simple, compound, complex, loose, periodic, and of course, short and long ones, but out of many, when we set down to write, one particular type of "sentence" requires our particular attention and effort—the topic sentence.

Analogically, working out topic sentences is like, in a way, creating a system of signs in a theme park for the purpose of assisting visitors in their tour of the park. Functionally, they work to the same purpose. Even if some visitors enjoy wandering around and enjoy whatever comes their way, and still have a good time, readers of your writing do expect topic sentences in almost each and every paragraph, which serve like the attractive signs in Disneyland.

Whatever type of sentences as mentioned above can serve the purpose of a topic sentence. Topic sentences can be as simple as "Our university is a good one" or as complex as "If history and literature are both texts, then literature is potentially as much as a context for history as history is for literature." They can be used to either start a paragraph or conclude a paragraph. For as a budding writer, placing the topic sentence at the beginning of a paragraph serves your purpose more directly. When you are progressing in your writing skills, you might be able to place your topic sentence in the middle of a paragraph.

Warm-Up Exercise: *Reading and Discussion*

Directions: Read the following sample essay carefully, and identify the topic sentence in each paragraph. If there is no topic sentence to be located in a paragraph, write one yourself. And then work in small groups to discuss on positions, features, and functions of topic sentences.

Beauty Is in the Eye of the Beholder

By Lorie Panipinto

For years men and women have been getting married. They say their wedding vows which bring them together as one. They promise to love and cherish each other until death does them apart.

When a man and a woman get married, it is one of the biggest decisions that they will make in life. A man may select a woman because he, in his own eyes, sees her as the just-right wife for him. Every man has his own definition of what the "just-right" wife is. For instance, the millionaire man and the poor man both may define their just-right wife according to her physical qualities.

A millionaire may describe his "just-right" wife as charming, beautiful, sexy, intelligent, and well developed. On the other hand, a poor man may define his "just-right" wife as pleasing, attractive, desirable, knowledgeable and shapely. Both men describe their just-right wife by the same physical qualities but use different words. The millionaire's definition of the just-right wife is more elegant, whereas the poor man's definition is a more common, everyday description.

Although some men define the just-right wife by her physical qualities, other men describe their just-right wife by her athletic qualities. For example, the outdoors man may define his just-right wife as a woman who loves to fish, to camp, to hunt, and to water ski, whereas the inside sportsman may define his just-right wife as a woman who enjoys watching football, basketball, baseball, and wrestling. Both of these men define their just-right wife by her sports qualities but in two different atmospheres.

Still, there are other men who have their definitions of the just-right wife. For instance, consider the fit man and the fat man. The fit man may describe his just-right wife as a woman who gets up every weekday morning at six o'clock and runs two to three miles. After running, she prepares breakfast, washes the dishes, takes the children to school, and then goes to work. After work, she arrives home, washes a couple of loads of laundry, goes to exercise class, picks the children up from school on her way home, and then cooks dinner. After dinner, she cleans the kitchen, bathes the children, and puts them to bed.

On the other hand, the fat man defines his just-right wife as a woman who gets up at eight o'clock in the morning, takes the children to McDonald's for breakfast, and drops them off at school. She then comes back home and lies on the couch watching soap operas all day. The children have to walk home from school in the afternoon. When they arrive at home, she instructs them to clean the house, do the laundry, and fix some hotdogs for dinner. Both men define their just-right wife with qualities that they admire within themselves.

Men from all nationalities also have their definition of the just-right wife. For example, the Italian man describes his woman as a woman who stands six feet one-inch tall with blonde hair and blue eyes, and who is well developed in the upper portion of her body. On the other hand, the French man may describe his ideal woman as a woman who stands only five feet three inches with brown hair and green eyes, and who is moderately built.

Other nationalities, such as the German man and the Spanish man may define their just-right wife as a woman with/in style: The German man may describe his just-right wife as a woman who likes to drive expensive sports cars, a woman who visits a different country every month and wears only the most expensive designer clothing, but the Spanish man may define his just-right wife as a woman who enjoys giving dinner parties every weekend, wearing a lot of jewelry, and drinking expensive wines.

In addition to the other men's definition of the just-right wife: the bachelor also has definition. He says that the just-right wife is someone else's wife. He picks her up in a bar, takes her to his house, and takes her home in the morning. The bachelor has no real definition for the just-right wife. That is why he is still a bachelor.

Section **O**ne: Definition of Topic Sentence

A topic sentence is a sentence that sets out the main idea or topic of a paragraph. It maps out the direction of a paper and allows the reader to see where each paragraph is heading. It shows the reader how the paragraph will relate to the thesis and specifically what topic within the thesis will be detailed, argued or explained.

A topic sentence can be broken into two parts: the topic and the controlling idea. The topic lets the readers know the general domain of the paragraph. While the controlling idea narrows the domain to the specific idea. The following sentence is an example of a topic sentence with a controlling idea: "Email has become an important part of my life." The topic of this sentence is "email," and the controlling idea is "an important part of my life."

A qualified topic sentence must be a complete sentence, not a fragment. It summarizes the entirety of the subject discussed in the paragraph; it has a clear, direct relationship to the thesis; it does not introduce a subject that is too complex or too simple to be covered in a paragraph, and it is fully supported by the remaining sentences in the paragraph.

Case Study

Directions: Analyze the given three cases below and summarize the functions of the topic sentences.

Case One

There are three reasons why Canada is one of the best countries in the world. First, Canada has an excellent health care system. All Canadians have access to medical services at a reasonable price. Second, Canada has a high standard of education. Students are taught by well-trained teachers and are encouraged to continue studying at university. Finally, Canada's cities are clean and efficiently managed. Canadian cities have many parks and lots of space for people. As a result, Canada is a desirable place to live in.

Case Two

Several Shakespearian characters were ruined by their desires for power. Cassius was one such character. He overthrew Julius Caesar to possess the emperor's power but died by having Pindarus, his slave, stab him with the same sword he had used to kill Caesar. Macbeth was another power—hungry character. To take over the crown, he assassinated his king, only to be killed later by Macduff. Edmund in <u>King Lear</u> was also ruined by an unnatural desire for power. After gaining his father's title and fortune through lies and intrigues, Edmund was killed by his triumphant brother, the lawful heir.

Case Three

<u>The unimportance Americans assign to the languages of others has caused problems in several areas.</u> The government has certainly had some red-faced officials because of inept translators. One especially embarrassing case is that of the State Department official who accompanied President Jimmy Carter to Poland. When during the course of a speech President Carter told the Polish people that he loved them, this interpreter assured the Poles that the American president Lusted after them. The journalistic world has also had its share of problems because of international reporters who could not speak the language of the country they were covering. For instance, some reporters covering the takeover of the American embassy in Iran could not speak Farsi; thus, their foreign interpreters controlled everything the press covered. The ineptness of American business in the use of the languages of others is perhaps responsible in part for the poor showing of American products on the international market. Because of their inability to use the languages of others, advertisers have made such stupid blunders as advertising a writing pen in South America as a product to prevent unwanted pregnancies and as claiming in Germany that a soft drink could restore life to the dead. The government, the press, and the business world could create a much better image of America and Americans by placing more emphasis on the importance of learning the languages of others.

Section Two: Positions of Topic Sentence

A topic sentence is often the first sentence in a paragraph especially when arguing a point where it may well be followed by further information, examples, etc. If the topic sentence is the second sentence, the first sentence will be a transitional sentence, a statement that bridges the idea of the previous paragraph to the idea in the paragraph at hand. If the writing is exploring a point, it frequently comes as the last sentence, drawing a conclusion from the argument. Occasionally the topic sentence is in the middle of a paragraph, when the paragraph moves from a general to a specific statement.

Topic Sentence at the Beginning

Sample: The punishment of criminals has always been a problem for society. Citizens have had to decide whether offenders such as first-degree murderers should be killed in a gas chamber, imprisoned for life, or rehabilitated and given a second chance in society. Many citizens argue that serious criminals should be executed. They believe that killing criminals will set an example for others and also rid society of a cumbersome burden. Other citizens say that no one has the right to take a life and that capital punishment is not a deterrent to crime. They believe that society as well as the criminal is responsible for the crimes and that killing the criminal does not solve the problems of either society or the criminal.

Topic Sentence in the Middle

Sample: Californians and Englanders are both American. They speak the same language and abide by the same federal laws. But they are very different in their ways of life. Mobility/dynamic—both physical and psychological—has made a great impression on the culture of Californians. Lack of mobility is the mark of the customs and morality of New Englanders.

Topic Sentence at the End

Sample: Americans might be embarrassed because their Japanese friends are so formal with them. Japanese might feel insulted because American acquaintances greet them casually. Still, the forms of greeting in both countries only show respect for others. It just happens that Americans and Japanese have a different way of looking at human relationships and thus have a different way of showing respect.

The Topic Sentence at both the Beginning and at the End

Sample: Good manners are important in all countries, but ways of expressing good manners are different from country to country. Americans eat with knives and forks, Japanese eat with chopsticks. Americans say "Hi" when they meet; Japanese bow. Many American men open doors for women; Japanese men do not. On the surface, it appears that good manners in America are not good manners in Japan, and in a way this is true, but in all countries it is good manners to behave considerately toward others and bad manners not to. It is only the way of behaving politely that differs from country to country.

Section Three: Features of Topic Sentence— the Controlling Idea

The topic sentence is the most general statement in the paragraph, however, not just any general statement can function as a qualified topic sentence. A topic sentence contains a controlling idea that commits the paragraph to a particular topic or subject. In simple terms, *a controlling idea* is a word or a phrase that tells precisely what the paragraph is about. Think of it as the program word or phrase. To learn the expected content of your favorite television program, you look in a television guide. The guide announces in a sentence or less the content of a thirty-minute show or an hour program. Your controlling idea functions in the same way. It is the word or phrase in the topic sentence that announces to your readers what they can expect in your paragraph. But more importantly, it gives you a clear idea of what you are going to articulate.

The controlling ideas in the topic sentences below are underlined:

College students are put to have access to various sources in their study.

Cross-culture communication <u>differs greatly</u> from that within the same culture.

China has made <u>a great deal of progress</u> in higher education in the last two decades.

Analysis：The first one commits the writer to discuss the various sources that students have access to in their study. The second indicates that the writer will discuss the difference between cross-culture and non-cross-culture communication. The third one requires the writer to describe the great deal of progress China has made in higher education in the last 20 years.

Tips：There are mainly two principles to keep in mind as you compose a topic sentence with a controlling idea.

Principle One

The controlling idea must be a word or phrase you can develop（not too broad/not too specific/but to give you space to develop）. It expresses your attitude or states what you are going to explain. If you select "London University is a good university" as your topic sentence, what are you going to write about? You might revise the sentence and add a word or phrase that you can explain as enlisted below：

The campus of London University is beautiful.

The faculty of London University is qualified.

The facilities of London University are up-to-date.

As illustrated above, it is important to well phrase the controlling idea. If a topic sentence lacks a well-phrased controlling idea, you may construct a paragraph that lacks unity and purpose. But when you begin with a topic sentence that has a well-stated controlling idea, you have a signpost to direct you through the paragraph.

Principle Two

The controlling idea must be as specific as you can make it. Try to limit or narrow your subject and attitude by choosing the most exact words possible. Use a specific word instead of a general one. For example, if you say "There is a book on my desk," the reader might wonder whether you mean a textbook, or a fiction.

Being specific is necessary for several reasons：

If you are specific, the reader will know what you mean.

If you are specific, you have a better chance of proving your point.

If you are specific, you can make the body of the paragraph more concrete.

Mini-task One

Directions: Underline the controlling idea in each of the topic sentences below.

1. I choose to live in the dorm because there are three reasons that lead me to do so.
2. Americans and Japanese have a different way of looking at human relationships and thus have a different way of showing respect.
3. Foreign custom is much stricter than Chinese custom in the matter of replying to invitations.
4. Different gestures may express the same idea in different cultures.
5. Although most major universities rely on college admission examinations, educators point out that they fail to identify certain important qualities.
6. To be accepted at Chicago University, student must follow established procedures.
7. Swedish scientists have proposed a new method of treating alcoholism.
8. Fast food restaurants are getting increasingly popular in China because of their convenience and low price.
9. Cancer patients anticipate some major breakthroughs in the treatment of the disease.
10. My brother, Joe, on the other hand, looks more conservative than Nick.
11. Those entering the job market for the first time have devised innovative methods to find employment.
12. My view on the negative effects of some advertisements.
13. It is generally believed that Chinese food can be classified into four types.
14. The ability to write good reports will be useful to you as students and professionals.
15. A dog does not make a good apartment pet.

Mini-task Two

Directions: Locate the topic sentence in each of the following paragraphs.

Paragraph One

Eating lunch is one of my favorite pastimes. Because lunch comes in the middle of the day, it gives me a welcome break from studying. At school, lunch means thirty minutes out of class and a chance to rest after the morning's work. While eating, I can plan what I'm going to do in the afternoon. And besides offering a pleasant break in the day, lunch is always a good meal.

The topic sentence for Paragraph One is _____

Paragraph Two

Foreign custom is much stricter than Chinese custom in the matter of replying to invitations. When you receive an invitation you should answer it immediately, saying definitely whether you are able to accept it or not. This is because the hostess probably wants to have a certain number of guests at her table and if you cannot come she will want to ask someone else. And it is not polite to ask anyone at the last minute. So you should let her know just as soon as possible whether you can come or not.

The topic sentence for Paragraph Two is _____

Paragraph Three

In this society, there are many professions for us to choose from. For example, we can be a worker, an instructor, a clerk, a novelist, a journalist, a doctor, a sailor or a nurse. Among them, I like teaching the most. Therefore, when I grow up, I wish to become an instructor. To be an instructor, I can serve the people. Our instructor is a good instructor and she sets us a good example. As teaching is a noble profession, many people like to take it. But teaching is a very demanding job. Instructors need to have a wide range of knowledge. Therefore, I must work hard in all my subjects. I should remember the saying, "Knowledge is a matter of science, and no dishonesty or conceit whatever is permissible. What it requires is definitely the opposite—honesty and modesty." I hope I can become a successful instructor. Do you think my wish is a meaningful one?

The topic sentence for Paragraph Three is _____

Paragraph Four

Parents and instructors are worried about the effect of television violence on children. Many children watch television for several hours every day, and even though they are watching children's programs, they are still confronted with scenes of violence and terror. Whether this constant exposure to violence encourages children to act more violently themselves is not certain. There has been a general increase in violence in society in recent years, but experts have not been able to trace this trend directly to television. Yet, they point out that the situation is dangerous because TV programs teach children at an early age to accept violence as a natural part of life.

The topic sentence for Paragraph Four is _____

Paragraph Five

My favorite class this semester is a speech class in argumentation. I like this class partly because the class offers me to read about current problems in the world, but mostly because it gives me the chance to exchange ideas with other students. Class discussions are especially interesting, and they may cover a range of topics from politics or science to art or religion. One meeting, for instance, stands out in my mind in which four students, one a Catholic, one a protestant, one a Jew, and one an atheist, give their different views on religion. That class was an eye-opener to me and made me think more deeply about my own views on the subject. I did not talk much in class that day because I was too busy listening, but on days when subjects I know more about are discussed, I talk quite a bit. Sometimes, we let all students work up about a topic in that class, and the arguments are always friendly. It is hard to fall asleep in my speech class because it demands much participation.

    The topic sentence for Paragraph Five is _____

Mini-task Three

Directions: Identify a topic of your choice and write three topic sentences to three paragraphs and then develop one of the topic sentences into a paragraph.

Homework

Task One

Directions: Read the following essay, and see if you can identify the topic sentences.

How to Improve Your Study Habits

    Perhaps you are an average student with average intelligence. You do well enough in school, but you probably think you will never be a top student. This is not necessarily the case, however. You can receive better grades if you want to. Yes, even students of average intelligence can be top students without additional work. Here's how:

    Plan your time carefully. Make a list of your weekly tasks. Then make a schedule or chart of your time. Fill in committed time such as eating, sleeping, meetings, classes, etc. then decide on good regular times for studying. Be sure to set aside enough time to complete your normal reading and work assignments. Of course, studying shouldn't occupy all of the free time on the schedule. It is important to set aside time for relaxation, hobbies, and entertainment as well. This weekly schedule may not solve all of your problems, but it will make you more aware of how you spend your time. Furthermore, it will enable you to plan your activities so that you have adequate time for both work and play.

Find a good place to study. Choose one place for your study area. It may be a desk or a chair at home or in the school library, but it should be comfortable, and it should not have distractions. When you begin to work, you should be able to concentrate on the subject.

Skim before you read. This means looking over a passage quickly before you begin to read it more carefully. As you preview the material, you get some idea of the content and how it is organized. Later when you begin to read you will recognize less important material and you may skip some of these portions. Skimming helps double your reading speed and improves your comprehension as well.

Make good use of your time in class. Listening to what the instructor says in class means less work later. Sit where you can see and hear well. Take notes to help you remember what the instructor says.

Study regularly. Go over your notes as soon as you can after class. Review important points mentioned in class as well as points you remain confused about. Read about these points in your textbook. If you know what the instructor will discuss the next day, skim and read that material, too. This will help you understand the next class. If you review your notes and textbook regularly, the material will become more meaningful and you will remember it longer. Regular review leads to improved performance on tests.

Develop a good attitude about tests. The purpose of a test is to show what you have learned about a subject. The world won't end if you don't pass a test, so don't worry excessively about a single test. Tests provide grades, but they also let you know what you need to spend more time studying and they help make your new knowledge permanent.

There are other techniques that might help you with your studying. Only a few have been mentioned here. You will probably discover many others after you have tried these. Talk with your classmates about their study techniques. Share with them some of the techniques you have found to be helpful. Improving your study habits will improve your grades.

Task Two: *Practice Writing Topic Sentences*

Directions: The paragraphs below do not have topic sentences. Read carefully and then write a topic sentence for these paragraphs respectively. Your topic sentence should have a controlling idea.

Paragraph One

In the West, we often try to build immediate rapport through humor, but of course, this is not universally seen to be appropriate in all contexts. The use of laughter can be experienced as a sign of disrespect by some, and so it is important to understand that this is another area where misunderstandings can be very likely to occur.

Paragraph Two

In some forms of communication, silence is to be expected before a response, as a sign of thoughtfulness and deference to the original speaker, yet at other times, silence may be experienced as a sign of hostility. In the West, twenty seconds of silence during a meeting is an extraordinarily long time, and people will feel uncomfortable with that. Someone invariably will break in to end the uncomfortable silence. But the same customs around silence are not universal.

Paragraph Three

Small cars may be more easily parked than large cars. In one major city, a traffic patrolman recently hauled two Volkswagen owners before a magistrate for parking their small cars in a single space and thereby cheating the city out of a quarter. The magistrate disagreed with the patrolman and commended the two car owners for their ingenuity. Small cars are better vehicles for icy weather. Seldom are they trapped by snow or mud, and they almost never lose their traction on icy grades. Finally, small cars are less expensive to operate. They get better gasoline mileage than their large counterparts and their tires and other accessories cost less than those for larger cars.

Paragraph Four

Firstborn children and only child tend to be leaders. Researchers have found that they dominate their younger brothers and sisters, have more self-esteem, and appear to be more adult-oriented. Twenty-one of the original twenty-three astronauts were either first-born or only children. Children who are born in the middle tend to be passive. They are average students and often dominated by both older and younger siblings. Last-born children have the highest social intelligence quotients. They are more verbal and tend to be more popular with their peers than are their older brothers and sisters.

Paragraph Five

One group of environmentalists is trying to save the California condor by captive breeding. Biologists in this group find condor nests in the wild and then remove an egg from the nest in an effort to force the adult birds to lay another. Several of these eggs have been successfully hatched. The scientists hope that these nestlings will breed in captivity when they mature. The opponents of captive breeding propose that the condor be saved by cleaning up the bird's environment. They argue that pesticides, lead, and power lines are responsible for its population decline. According to them, if these three things were removed from the bird's habitat, it could exist and prosper in the wild.

Paragraph Six

On the first day of their Mexico City vacation, tourists may go to Chapultepec Castle and view the many treasures of Maximilian and Carlota. They may spend the next two or three days going through the National Museum of Anthropology. There they can study the various cultures of the prehistoric as well as later Indian cultures of the area. Then, they may wish to spend a day touring the other famous museums and the historic churches of the city. Before they fly back to the United States, they will want to devote one day to a drive about thirty miles northeast of the city to visit the Pyramid of the Sun and the Pyramid of the Moon.

Paragraph Seven

Some penguins, like humans, keep the same mate for several years. Also like people, these birds of the Antarctic region live in colonies. In fact, they are sometimes so crowded together that they barely have room for their nests. In addition, penguin domestic life is like the domestic life of many humans in that both parents care for the young. Penguins also enjoy fun. For example, they often ride on floes for no other reason than pleasure. Swimming together is another activity they enjoy. Finally, some of the birds of the South Pole, like some humans, are thieves. They steal from each other the pebbles used for nest-building. When one bird catches another in the act, a great disturbance resembling a human quarrel ensues.

Paragraph Eight

If a mediator is of the same culture or nationality as one of the disputants, but not the other, this gives the appearance of bias, even when none exists. Even when bias is not intended, it is common for mediators to be more supportive or more understanding of the person who is of his or her own culture, simply because they understand them better. Yet when the mediator is of a third cultural group, the potential for cross-cultural misunderstandings increases further. In this case engaging in extra discussions about the process and the manner of carrying out the discussions is appropriate, as is extra time for confirming and re-confirming understandings at every step in the dialogue or negotiating process.

Task Three: Write an Essay with a Topic Sentence Leading Each Paragraph

Directions: The topic will be of your own choice and interest. The length requirement is around 200 words.

Unit Five

Defining

要点提示：定义法是最常用的写作方法之一,小到解释一个生词,大至阐述自由、民主与人权,我们无一不在运用定义的方法解析概念、界定术语。根据定义对象的不同,定义的方法可繁可简。由简至繁可将定义法排序为词语→句子→段落→文章四种类别。每一类别均有其各自不同的定义方法,需要我们认真学习,深刻领会,最终做到运用自如。

Introductory Remarks

Knowing how to define a term is one of the most valuable skills you can learn—not just as a student of English or math or psychology, but also as you experience life. The more you learn about life, the more you realize that relationships between people are often permanently destroyed because of "misunderstandings." These misunderstandings are sometimes the direct result of one's failure to communicate his or her meaning of a word. For example, consider the case of Pam. Pam is eighteen years old. She wants to leave home and move into an apartment because her parents aren't giving her enough "freedom." Pam's parents, however, are firmly convinced that Pam is already getting too much "freedom." Obviously, Pam and her parents have different definitions of the word "freedom." Perhaps, if Pam had clearly defined what she meant by "freedom," the conflict with her parents could have been peacefully resolved. A clear, thorough definition of a term at the outset of a disagreement can prevent a minor disagreement from exploding into a major war.

Warm-Up Exercises

Exercise One: *Reading and Defining*

Directions：Read the following passage and define the underlined terms.

Definition of Tourism

Tourism is the attraction of the other：other places，times，peoples，practices. Without the attraction of the other，tourism does not really exist. The other，the exotic，may have its roots in the culture，history，or natural landscapes of an area and its people. In China，foreign tourists come not to relax but to experience scenic beauty，historical treasures，and cultural activities.

Developing countries have seen international tourism as a relatively quick way to garner foreign capital. Tourism，as the smokeless，clean，and green industry，is said to make fewer demands on the resources of developing countries. The World Bank has made loans for tourism development，especially for roads，airports，water，sewage，and other infrastructural improvements.

Besides its cultural and economic dimension，tourism can also have a political dimension. A country uses tourism to present its positive qualities. For China，tourism has provided an opportunity to showcase its economic strengths and political wisdom，and to increase positive foreign perception.

There is not just one geography of tourism，but many. Start with the raw materials：places to go，sights to see. Then consider the world's tourism consumers：people from countless cultural backgrounds，with money，curiosity，or longing.

Is tourism good for a place? Is it an appropriate way to bring new wealth to a community，region or country? As one author has asked，is tourism a "passport to development?" The answer depends on the consequences—economic benefits of tourism must be weighed against the socio-cultural costs. For example，tourists travel by the busload to a remote community to admire a traditional way of life，and their money is very welcome；but the local community finds itself having to perform its sacred ceremonies six times a day for camera-carrying outsiders；and the money replaces tradition with conveniences. Does tourism destroy the very object it desires?

Geographers studying tourism try to answer this question，examining efforts to create tourism-based development, the stages of development, and the socio-cultural effects.

(From *China at the Crossroad*)

Exercise Two

Directions: Discuss in small groups the following terms. Each group is expected to work out a definition to the terms respectively by providing one word, one sentence or one paragraph.

1. mobile phone
2. market economy
3. a family home
4. interpersonal skills
5. personnel manager
6. harmonious society

Section One: Introduction to Word Level Definition

In writing or speaking, you often need to provide your reader or listener with one word definition—the easiest way to explain a word in terms of another word, a synonym, which means the same or nearly the same, e. g, "Dr. Andrews was indeed loquacious, an extremely talkative man."

You should always include a brief definition when the word or term that you use might not be understood by the reader. Also, make sure that the language of your definition is simpler than the original term. The following version would only create more confusion: "Dr. Andrew was indeed loquacious, an extremely garrulous man."

Always consider your reader's ability to comprehend what you are writing; be aware of readers' limitations, but don't insult their intelligence by oversimplifying terms or ideas that they would obviously understand.

Mini-task

Directions: Write down the explanation to the words or expressions in terms of another word or expression with similar meaning (by using synonyms). For example: secure—safe; mobile phone—cell phone.

1. Let's get the clock ticking.
2. He is a positive instructor.
3. Women hold up half of the sky.

4. She is an outstanding student.

5. best top models

6. sunrise industry

7. wanted advertisement

8. unidentified murders

9. personality trait

10. back on track

Section Two: Introduction to Sentence Level Definition

Here is a pattern to follow in writing sentence level definitions:

term + class + feature / differentiation

First, place the term to be defined in a class of category: for example, fascism is an economic system. This places the term in a general class; you are saying that fascism (the term) belongs to a limited class of things (economic systems).

Second, describe the principal characteristics that distinguish or differentiate the term from all others in the class: for example, fascism is an economic system in which industry is wholly controlled by the central government while ownership remains in private hands.

Examples of Sentence Level Definition

1. a bus stop (term to be defined)—a place (class/classification) where people get on and out of or waiting for a bus (differentiation/differences)

2. a car phone—a cellular telephone for use in a motor vehicle

3. a bypass operation—an operation in which a diseased or obstructed segment of the circulatory or digestive systems of the body is circumvented

4. a cash card—a card which allows one to perform certain banking activities via an ATM(automatic teller machine)

5. a cashless society—a society which doesn't purchase goods or services by means of hard currency but rather by credit card, electronic funds transfer, etc.

6. a university instructor—a person who teaches in colleges or universities

7. a school—a place where you go to learn, to gain knowledge by instruction and study

8. child abuse—mistreatment of a child by a parent or guardian, which may take the form of

physical or psychological ill-treatment, neglect or sexual molestation

9. convenience-food-product—especially a food product, which is designed to save time and effort for the consumer in cooking or preparation

Such examples enable us to safely draw a conclusion that a sentence level definition consists of three parts: term to be defined, category to which the term belongs, and specific detail which differentiates it from other terms in the category. Note that both the category and the differentiating detail must be as exact as possible: for instance, we don't say, "A bus stop is a place," but "A bus stop is a place where people wait for or get out of a bus."

In addition, your specific detail must provide enough information to distinguish your term from any other term that could fall in the same category. For example, it is inadequate to say that "Love is a strong feeling that one person has for another," because you are not differentiating love from other strong feelings. Think of some other terms that would apply to this definition:

Hatred is a strong feeling that one person has for another.

Passion is a strong feeling that one person has for another.

Sympathy is a strong feeling that one person has for another.

How would you rewrite this definition so that it would apply only to the term "love"?

Mini-task

Directions: Write one-sentence definitions to the following terms.

1. environmental friendly
2. family planning policy
3. individualism
4. information age
5. rule of law

Section Three: Introduction to Extended Definition

Lots of terms represent concepts and ideas that are too complicated to be defined in one word or one sentence; therefore, a paragraph is necessary to explain the meaning. For example, by saying "Love is a strong feeling that one has for another," you are not differentiating love from other strong feelings such as hate, sympathy, and passion. This definition of "love" would have to be expanded before you could fully understand the meaning of "love." In other words, you would need an extended definition of this term, which follows the same three-part structure: topic sentence + extended definition + conclusion.

Topic sentence: Introduction to the controlling idea in the definition. Your topic sentence will usually have as its subject the word to be defined. The defination should be the general meaning you attach to the word. For instance, "Cultural relativity means respect for the ways of people who are different from ourselves," and "Justice is rewarding or punishing a person according to his deeds."

To introduce a topic, however, you need a paragraph to explain it. Remember that a topic sentence needs not only a subject but an attitude toward the subject. For example, "Different cultures have different interpretations to sexual harassment," "Love has different meanings for different people," and "Everybody has his side of the story about fair process," are actually unsatisfactory topic sentences. The following two sentences are qualified topic sentences:

- People of different ages and professions are doing physical exercises by the lake in the early morning.
- Traveling by train is a quite different experience in China than it is in the United States for the difference of services provided.

Body (extended definition): Development of the controlling idea through various methods of definition such as synonyms, examples, word origin, comparison and contrast, negation, and process.

Restatement of the controlling idea: At the end of the paragraph, you are expected to sum up your attitude toward the meaning of the term in your topic sentence, which you have already proved in the body.

Mini-task: *Reading and Discussion*

Directions: Read the extended definitions provided below, and discuss on the structure features of the definition paragraphs.

Paragraph One: Martin Luther King, Jr., defines the abstract term "power."

Power, properly understood, is the ability to achieve purpose. It is the strength required to bring about social, political, or economic changes. In this sense power is not only desirable but necessary in order to implement the demands of love and justice. One of the greatest problems of history is that the concepts of love and power are usually contrasted as polar opposites. Love is identified with a resignation of power and power with a denial of love. It was this misinterpretation that caused Nietzsche, the philosopher of the "will to power," to reject the Christian concept of love. It was this same misinterpretation which induced Christian theologians to reject Nietzsche's philosophy of the "will to power" in the name of the Christian idea of love. What is needed is a realization that power without love is reckless and abusive and that love without power is sentimental and anemic. Power at its best is love implementing the demands of justice...

Paragraph Two: Engagement

Engagement, as one of the three principles of fair process, means involving individuals in the decisions that affect them by asking their input and allowing them to refute the merits of one another's ideas and assumptions. Engagement communicates management's respect for individuals and their ideas. Encouraging refutation sharpens everyone's thinking and builds collective wisdom. Engagement results in better decisions by management and greater commitment from all involved in executing those decisions.

Paragraph Three: Explanation

Explanation, as one of the three principles of fair process, means that everyone involved and affected should understand why final decisions are made as they are. An explanation of the thinking underlying decisions makes people confident that managers have considered their opinions and have made those decisions impartially in the overall interests of the company. An explanation allows employees to trust manager's intentions even if their own ideas have been rejected. It also serves as a powerful feedback loop that enhances learning.

Section Four: Approaches to the Development of the Controlling Idea

The development of the controlling idea can be accomplished in a number of ways such as synonyms, examples, word origin, comparison and contrast, and negation.

Synonyms

A synonym, as previously explained, is a word that has almost the same meaning as another word. Hence, if you are defining *phobia*, words like *dread*, *panic*, *horror*, or *hysteria* might help the readers understand the meaning, especially if they are more familiar with these words than with *phobia*.

Examples

Examples often help to clarify the meaning of a word. Consequently, they often come in a definition paragraph. The reader will have a clearer understanding of the meaning of phobia if you provide specific examples of different kinds of phobias.

Word Origin

If you were defining *claustrophobia*, you could tell the reader that the word is derived from the Latin word *claustrium* meaning "lock, bar, bolt," and, later, "a shut-up place, a cell or cloister," and from the French word phobia, meaning "fearing" or "dreading." You could also show how the meaning of a word has changed throughout the course of history.

Comparison and / or Contrast

Even though a phobia is not as serious a disorder as paranoia, being in a phobia about something can be compared to/with being paranoia, because a person who suffers from paranoia often behaves much like an individual who has a particular phobia. For example, a person who has a paranoid persecution complex has such an irrational obsession about being persecuted that he or she begins to see danger in harmless situations and begins to see enemies everywhere—whether they exist or not.

Negation

Sometimes you can help the reader understand what something is by explaining what is not. For example, suppose your reader has three conceptions (A, B, C) of the word you are defining. If you show the reader that you are not talking about A, and you are not talking about B, then you are helping the reader determine the meaning of the term. Through the process of elimination, the reader narrows down his or her thinking to C, and thus are no longer confused about other possible meanings of the term.

Mini-task One: *Identifying Defining Methods*

Directions: Tell what method of defining is used in each of the following definitions.

1. Man is a two-legged animal without feathers.
2. Man comes from the Gothic manna, perhaps from the root word "man," which means "to think."
3. A man is a human being, a person.

4. Man is different from other animals in that he alone can communicate when not within sight or hearing of men. Man alone walks erect on two feet; most other animals have no free limbs. Man has an opposable thumb which allows him to pick up and hold things easily, whereas most animals have thumbs parallel to their other digits.

5. Man is not the only animal that thinks or the only animal that communicates. He is not born with a conscience nor is he born with complicated instincts to guide his future actions.

Mini-task Two: *Reading and Discussion*

Directions: Read the following passage, and then discuss in small groups how the author defines "stress" through the use of comparison, example, and process (a combination of different methods).

The word "stress," when applied to a combat situation, has a special meaning. It can refer to physical, emotional, or mental stress or any combination of the three. Physical stress, which is probably the easiest to understand, deals with the strain placed on the body during combat. It is an enormous demand placed on the soldier's energy, and it quickly stretches his physical resources to the limit. His adrenaline flows, and he can feel his heartbeat rapidly speeding up, and he becomes hyperactive with excessive strength and speed. Just as quickly, though, exhaustion sets in upon him, and all of his bumps, cuts and bruises begin to ache. This is often accompanied by a painful headache or a severe case of the shakes due to a rapid depletion of blood sugar. It is similar to running a foot race. One starts out at a fast pace, but in a short time, he tries, and all of his energy seems to be depleted. As one tries to continue running, he can feel every muscle in his body begin to throb. It is hard to tell sometimes where physical stress stops and emotional stress begins. Emotional stress includes fears, hate, sorrow, and even, at time, a curious form of joy. When the soldier is under duress, each of the emotions exerts its pressures upon him, sometimes causing panic or hysteria. For example, fear can be so powerful an influence that a soldier who gets caught in a fire fight can react by just starting to run, trying to escape, instead of immediately jumping for cover. He then becomes a running target for the enemy. One may wonder how joy can even be remotely connected to a combat situation, but, as all of the other pressures build up, laughter can become a form of release—a type of hysteria of its own. A man might find something funny that might be totally humorless to others and break out in a low rumbling laugh that turns into a long, rapturous convulsion. It can occur anytime, anywhere. Emotional stress in a combat situation can therefore be highly dangerous, but mental stress is probably the worse type of stress. It includes the pressures and strains caused by the mind's ability to think, to wonder, to remember, and to comprehend. It occurs when the soldier realizes that he may die or that he may not live up to what he expects of himself. It is seeing himself in a different way and wondering if he'll ever get home to live his life over and correct his mistakes. It is being responsible for another's life or perhaps many lives and living with the worry and the guilt. Mental stress can also be generated by memories of home and what mom and dad expect him to be. He may try to fulfill their expectation and crack under the strain. Poor living conditions also contribute to mental stress—in addition to the continuous presence of the nagging, unanswered question: "why am I here?" Actually, one could take all life's stresses, multiply them by two, and force them on an individual for an hour; then he would experience what a soldier in combat experiences in two minutes. Stress, when applied to a combat situation, clearly has a meaning all its own.

(By Mark Pleshenko)

Mini-task Three: *In-class Writing Practice*

Directions: Define two of the following abstract terms in clear and well-developed paragraphs.

passion	honesty	trust	marriage
courage	mercy	wealth	frustration
kindness	comfortable	friendship	freedom
luck	punishment	education	religion
work	peace	family	hate
equality	happiness	hope	sorrow

Homework

Task One: Reading and Response

Directions: Read the following essays, and analyze the definition devices used in any one of the passages in about 100 words.

Passage One

On Beauty

By Kahlil Gibran

Where shall you seek beauty, and how shall you find her unless she herself be your way and your guide? And how shall you speak of her except she be the weaver of your speech?

The aggrieved and the injured say, "Beauty is kind and gentle. Like a young mother half-shy of her own glory she walks among us."

And the passionate say, "Nay, beauty is a thing of might and dread. Like the tempest she shakes the earth beneath us and the sky above us."

The tired and the weary say, "Beauty is of soft whisperings. She speaks in our spirit. Her voice yields to our silences like a faint light that quivers in fear of the shadow."

But the restless say, "We have heard her shouting among the mountains, and with her cries came the sound of hoofs, and the beating of wings and the roaring of lions."

At night the watchmen of the city say, "Beauty shall rise with the dawn from the east."

And at noontime the toilers and the wayfarers say, "We have seen her leaning over the earth from the windows of the sunset."

In winter, say the snow-bound, "She shall come with the spring leaping upon the hills."

And in the summer heat the reapers say, "We have seen her dancing with the autumn leaves, and we saw a drift of snow in her hair."

All these things have you said of beauty, yet in truth you spoke not of her but of needs unsatisfied, and beauty is not a need but an ecstasy. It is not a mouth thirsting nor an empty hand stretched forth, but rather a heart enflamed and a soul enchanted. It is not the image you would see nor the song you would hear, but rather an image you see though you close your eyes and a song you hear though you shut your ears. It is not the sap within the furrowed bark, nor a wing attached to a claw, but rather a garden forever in bloom and a flock of angels forever in flight.

Beauty is life when life unveils her holy face.

Passage Two

Hobby

A hobby can be almost anything a person likes to do when he has time to spare. Hobbyists raise pets, build model ships, weave baskets, or carve soap figures. They watch birds, hunt animals, climb mountains, raise flowers, fish, ski, skate, and swim. Hobbyists also paint pictures, attend concerts and plays, and perform on musical instruments. They collect everything from books to butterflies and from shells to stamps.

People take up hobbies because these activities offer enjoyment, friendship, knowledge, and relaxation. Sometimes they even yield financial profit. Hobbies help people relax after periods of hard work, and provide a balance between work and play. Hobbies also offer interesting activities for persons who have retired. Anyone rich or poor, old or young, sick or well, can follow a satisfying hobby, regardless of his age, position or income.

Hobbies can help a person's mental and physical health. Doctors have found that hobbies are valuable in helping patients recover from physical or mental illness. Hobbies give bedridden or wheelchair patients something to do, and provide interests that keep them from thinking about themselves. Many hospitals treat patients by having them take up interesting hobbies or pastimes.

In early times, most people were too busy making a living to have many hobbies. But some persons who had leisure did enjoy hobbies. The ancient Egyptians played games with balls made of wood, pottery, and papyrus. Some Greeks and Romans collected miniature soldiers.

People today have more time than ever before for hobbies. Machines and automation have reduced the amount of time they must spend on their jobs. Hobbies provide variety for workers who do the same monotonous tasks all day long. More people are retiring than ever before, and at an earlier age. More people need to worry about what to do with their newly-found leisure hours.

Sir William Osier, a famous Canadian doctor, expressed the value of hobbies by saying, "No man is really happy or safe without a hobby, and it makes precious little difference what the outside interest may be—botany, beetles, or butterflies; roses, tulips, or irises; fishing, mountaineering, or antiques—anything will do so long as he straddles a hobby and rides it hard."

Passage Three

Happiness

Happiness can be described as a positive mood and a pleasant state of mind.

According to recent polls sixty to seventy percent of Americans consider themselves to be moderately happy and one in twenty persons feels very unhappy. Psychologists have been studying the factors that contribute to happiness. It is not predictable whether a person in an apparently ideal situation is necessarily happy. The ideal situation may have little to do with his actual feelings.

A good education and income are usually considered necessary for happiness. Though both may contribute, they are only chief factors if the person is seriously undereducated or actually suffering from lack of physical needs.

The rich are not likely to be happier than the middle-income group or even than those with very low incomes. People with college education are somewhat happier than those who do not graduate from high school, and it is believed that this is mainly because they have more opportunities to control their lives. Yet people with a high income and a college education may be less happy than those with the same income and no college education.

Poor health does not rule out happiness except for the severely weakened or those in pain, but learning to cope with a health problem can contribute to happiness. Love has a higher correlation with happiness than any other factors.

It should be noted that people quickly get used to what they have, and they are happiest when they feel they are increasing their level no matter where it stands at a given time.

The best formula for happiness is to be able to develop the ability to tolerate frustration, to have a personal involvement and commitment, and to develop self-confidence and self-esteem.

Task Two: Writing Practice

Directions: Write one-sentence definitions to the terms given below.

1. a positive teacher
2. an outstanding student
3. co-culture
4. triangle love
5. head-hunter

Task Three: Writing Practice

Directions: Define two of the following abstract terms in clear and well-developed paragraphs.

passion	honesty	trust	marriage
courage	mercy	wealth	frustration
kindness	comfortable	friendship	freedom
luck	punishment	education	religion
work	peace	family	hate
equality	happiness	hope	sorrow

Unit Six
Comparing and Contrasting

第六单元　　比较对照法

要点提示：比较与对照虽常常混用,但比较往往注重的是相同点,对照则关注不同点。比较对照写作的一般方法为:首段——主题句段落,告知读者拟比较或对照的对象和关注的重点(相同点或不同点);中间段——推展主题句段落。常用的推展方法有两种,即交替比较法(A/B/A/B…)和分类阐述法(一段专述 A,另一段专述B);尾段——概括归纳已经比较或对照的内容。

Introductory Remarks

One of the best ways to make a subject interesting and informative is to develop it by means of comparison or contrast. Comparison shows similarities between persons, places, things, ideas, or situations. Contrast does just the opposite：it points out the differences between persons, places, things, ideas, or situations. Whether you organize material for a comparison or for a contrast, your methods are essentially the same.

Warm-Up Exercise：Reading and Discussion

Directions：Read the two passages given below and discuss in small groups the methods of comparison and contrast writing. Each group is expected to work out a list of the writing skills and report the list to the class.

Passage One

Alfred Nobel—a Man of Many Contrasts

Alfred Nobel, the Swedish inventor and industrialist, was a man of many sharp contrasts. He was the son of a bankrupt, but became a millionaire; a scientist with a love of literature, an industrialist who managed to remain an idealist. He made a fortune but lived a simple life, and although cheerful in company he was often sad in private. A lover of mankind, he never had a wife or family to love him; a patriotic son of his native land, he died alone on foreign soil. He invented a new explosive dynamite to improve the peacetime industries of mining and road building, but saw it used as a weapon of war to kill and injure his fellow men.

Passage Two

Newspapers

In some countries as many as nine out of ten adults read at least one newspaper a day. Seen in purely business terms, few products can ever have been so successful in reaching as much of their potential market. Why do so many people read newspaper?

There are five basic functions of a newspaper: to inform, to comment, to persuade, to instruct and to entertain. You may well think that this list of functions is in order of importance but, if so, you would not be in agreement with the majority of the reading public. Of the two broad categories of newspaper the popular and the quality, the former have a readership of millions, while the latter, only hundreds of thousands. Yet the popular papers seem largely designed for entertainment, with quizzes, competitions, cartoons, and light-hearted human interest stories. Their news coverage contains a lot of comment and persuasive language; the information content is rather low, and instruction is very minor. The quality newspapers put a much lower one on entertainment.

It is not in content that the two types of paper differ. There is a difference, too, in the style in which the articles are written. The popular papers generally use more dramatic language with a lot of wordplay, and their journalists tend to use shorter sentences and avoid less well-known vocabulary. This means that popular newspapers are easier for a native speaker to understand, though probably not for a non-native speaker.

In order to decide whether a newspaper is a quality or a popular one, it is not even necessary to read it, since you can tell simply by the way it looks. Popular papers are generally smaller with fewer columns per page. They have bigger headlines and more photographs. There is a greater variety of typeface and printed symbols. The articles are shorter and there are fewer per page.

Such devices are not only used to make the paper more attractive; they may also influence what the reader reads. Large headlines, pictures and position on the page all serve to draw the reader's attention to one article rather than another.

Since popular newspapers have a much large readership than the apparently more neutral quality paper, it may be fair to conclude that the average reader not only wants to be entertained by a newspaper, but prefers his reading to be guided and opinions given to him.

Section One: Topic Sentence Writing for Comparison and Contrast

The topic sentence of a comparison or contrast is of primary importance because the writer's purpose must be clearly defined and stated. Your topic sentence, therefore, should identify both items (subjects) to be compared or contrasted, and tell the reader exactly what you are going to say about these items (attitude). Again, remember to narrow your topic sentence so that your purpose is clear to the reader and so that you can prove your topic sentence with specific details.

When developing the topic sentence into a paragraph (which also serves as the topic sentence paragraph), the writer should tell the reader what he is going to compare and contrast as well as what he is going to emphasize. If the writer puts emphases on the similarities, he should mention the differences, and vice versa. Transition words such as *but*, *however*, *on the contrast*, *while*, etc., are frequently used in comparison and contrast composition to achieve coherence.

Example One: *My Brothers Nick and Joe*

Both my brothers, Nick and Joe, have the same parents and the same background, but they differ considerably in appearance and lifestyle.

Analysis:

What is the writer going to compare and contrast? —His two brothers, Nick and Joe.

What is the writer going to emphasize? —His two brothers' difference in appearance and lifestyle.

What similarities have been mentioned? —The same parents and the same background.

What connectors have been used? —*Both*, *but*.

Example Two: *Where to Live—in a City or in a Village?*

Although life in a village benefits people in a variety of ways such as being far away from dirt and noise, more quiet and peaceful, less crimes, less traffic and less pollution, people in a village are conservative and more friendly. I prefer to live in a city for it provides more opportunities for a successful career and all-around development.

Analysis:

From this topic sentence, we can see that the writer is going to make a contrast and comparison between the life in a village and that in a city. The advantages of city life are to be emphasized, therefore the writer has mentioned a few positive points of village life. "Although" is used to make the sentence read more smoothly.

Mini-task One: *Writing topic sentence paragraphs.*

Directions: Write a topic sentence paragraph on either of the two topics given below (no more than 60 words).

　　Topic One: Growing up in a Small Town or Growing up in a Large City

　　Topic Two: Working for a Large Company or Running Your Own Business

Mini-task Two: *Discuss your writing in sharing groups.*

Section Two: Two Basic Methods for Developing Comparison and Contrast Paragraphs with Topic Sentences

First Method: sentence to sentence development (point by point arrangement of ideas)

If you let A and B stand for the two things being compared, then you compare them point by point. Every time you say something about A, make sure that you also say something about B right in the sentence that immediately follows.

Sample of sentence to sentence development

My Mother and Father

There is an old saying that husbands and wives start to look and behave like each other after a while. I don't know if this was true of my mother and father. Both of my parents had brown hair and brown eyes and both had low voices and gentle personalities. My father, however, was eight years older than my mother and taller and thinner. He was built as straight as an arrow and his face was longer and more angular than my mother's. My mother was shorter than my father and had a rounder and fuller face and she looked as soft as a willow. My mother was quieter than my father and talked much less than he did. She was also a much neater and more patient person than my father. My father was more intelligent and more experienced in life than my mother. He was accustomed to doing everything quickly, from working to talking. My mother, on the other hand, worked and spoke much more slowly. My father was always early for an appointment, while my mother was usually late.

Second Method: paragraph to paragraph development (block arrangement of ideas)

If you let A and B stand for the two things being compared, then you can use the block method as your development strategy, namely, you start writing all about A in one paragraph, then all about B in another. Thus you present A in a block and B in another, and hence this is called "block method."

Keep in mind that these two development methods or patterns need not always be followed rigidly; experienced writers use the two essential methods alternately and creatively for the sole purpose of developing effective and interesting comparison or contrast paragraphs.

Sample of paragraph to paragraph development

My Brothers Nick and Joe

Both of my brothers, Nick and Joe, have the same parents and the same background, but they differ considerably in appearance and lifestyle.

Nick, the younger one, has long curly hair and a beard. He usually dresses casually in blue jeans and a T-shirt. He is a cook in a small restaurant. Because the restaurant is near his home, he rides his bicycle to work. In his free time, Nick goes to movies and plays football. He lives alone in the city in a small house.

My brother, Joe, on the other hand, looks more conservative than Nick. He has shorter, straighter hair. He has a moustache but no beard. His clothes are also more conservative than Nick's are. Because he is a businessman, he wears a suit and tie to work. He drives his car to his downtown office every day. In his spare time he goes dancing and plays soccer. Joe lives in a large house in the suburbs with his wife, their children, and a cat.

Case Study of the Two Methods

Topic: The Differences Between Airplanes and Helicopters

An Outline for Point by Point Arrangement

Paragraph One: Introduction wherein to state your purpose of discussing differences between airplanes and helicopters.

Paragraph Two: Differences between airplanes and helicopters

    A. Shape and design

        a. Airplanes

        b. Helicopters

    B. Speed

        a. Airplanes

        b. Helicopters

    C. Direction of takeoff and flight

        a. Airplanes

        b. Helicopters

Paragraph Three: Conclusion

Analysis:

This outline is developed by using point by point arrangement of ideas. In the beginning paragraph, you state what you are going to compare and contrast (the purpose of writing). In the second paragraph, you compare and contrast airplanes and helicopters point by point. Every time you say something about airplanes, you also say something about helicopters right in the sentence that immediately follows. Finally, you summarize as a conclusion the main points presented in Paragraph Two.

An Outline for Block Arrangement

Paragraph One: Introduction wherein to state your purpose of discussing differences between airplanes and helicopters

Paragraph Two: Airplanes

    A. Shape and design

    B. Speed

    C. Direction of takeoff and flight

Paragraph Three: Helicopters

    A. Shape and design

    B. Speed

    C. Direction of takeoff and flight

Paragraph Four: Conclusion

Analysis:

This outline is developed by using block method, namely, you start writing purpose of discussing differences between airplanes and helicopters in the beginning paragraph, and then you write all about airplanes in the second paragraph and helicopters in the third. Finally, you summarize the main points in Paragraph Two and Three.

Mini-task One

Directions: Examine the following short comparison or contrast essay, and decide whether the author uses block or point-by-point arrangement.

The Differences Between Airplanes and Helicopters

Airplanes and helicopters are both important forms of air travel, but there are great differences between them.

The first major difference between airplanes and helicopters is their shape and design. Airplanes, for example, have long, slender bodies with wings while helicopters have round bodies and propellers rather than wings.

Another difference between airplanes and helicopters is their speed. Airplanes can travel extremely fast, reaching speeds of over 1,875 miles (3,000 kilometers) per hour. Helicopters, on the other hand, are much slower than airplanes.

The final big difference between airplanes and helicopters is their direction of takeoff and flight. Airplanes take off horizontally and can only move in a forward direction. They need a lot of space for takeoff and landing. Airplanes regularly carry several hundred passengers. Helicopters, however, take off vertically and can move in any direction. Helicopters require a very small takeoff or landing space, and most helicopters carry only two to five passengers.

Because of the great differences between airplanes and helicopters, each is used for a specific purpose. Airplanes and helicopters, therefore, are both important forms of air travel.

Mini-task Two: *Writing a Comparison or Contrast Essay*

Directions: Suppose you are a personnel manager of ABC Company and you are recruiting a secretary. Choose one from the following two candidates and state your reasons.

Candidates Qualifications	Mary	Jane
Age	23	24
Education	Higher education English major	Higher education Chinese major
Working experience	No	2 years
Computer operation	Proficient	Proficient
Appearance	Beautiful	Plain

Mini-task Three: *Discussion and Presentation*

Directions: Discuss and select the best essay in your group. After the discussion, the writer of the essay is expected to read his or her paper to the whole class.

Homework

Task One: Writing Practice

Directions: Write an essay of comparison or contrast. Decide which method suits your subject better, and then write on one of the given topics. You are also expected to begin your paragraphs with qualified topic sentences, which meet the four essential requirements.

Your hometown and another place

Two close friends

Discipline by your mother and your father

Two vacations

Two of your instructors

Task Two: Reading

Directions: Read the passages given below and summarize the comparing and contrasting methods used respectively in each passage.

Passage One

Paris and Washington

Paris and Washington differ in age and population; however, anyone who has seen the two cities can tell that they are very similar.

Of course, Paris is much older than Washington. The French city is over 2,000 years old. Washington, in contrast, is very young. It is also much larger than Washington. Paris has more than 2,500,000 people. Washington has just over 700,000.

In spite of these differences, the similarities are striking. First, both cities are the political centers of their countries. The president of France lives in the heart of Paris, in the Eysees palace. Likewise, the president of the United States lives in the heart of Washington, in the White House. The French national assembly meets in Paris, in the Palais bourbon. The congress of the United State has its meeting on Capital Hill. Second, the two cities look similar. L' Enfant, the French engineer who designed Washington, was greatly influenced by the layout of the capital of France. For this reason, many of the buildings and monuments in Washington are symmetrically located in view of one another, just as they are in Paris. Both cities are also the sites of magnificent monuments, important historical landmarks, fine museums, beautiful parks, and broad, tree-lined avenues. Finally, tourism is as important for Washington as it is for Paris. Every year, millions of tourists from all parts of the world visit these cities to view their attractions.

Passage Two

Shopping

Shopping for clothes is not the same experience for a man as it is for a woman. A man goes shopping because he needs something. He knows what he wants, and his purpose is to find it and buy it, and the price is a less important consideration. All men simply walk into a shop and ask the assistant for what they want. If the shop has it, the salesman immediately introduces it, and the business of trying it on is done at once. All being well, the bargain can be and often is completed in less than five minutes, with hardly any chat and to everyone's satisfaction.

For a man, slight problems may begin when the shop does not have what he wants. Then the salesman tries to sell the customer something else—he offers the nearest he can to the item required. He usually says, "I know this jacket is not the style you want, sir, but would you like to try it on for size? It happens to be the color you wanted." Few men have patience with this treatment, and the usual reply is: "This is the right color and may be the right size, but I should be wasting my time and yours by trying it on."

Now how does a woman go about buying clothes? She does so in the opposite way. She has never fully made up her mind what she wants, and she is only "having a look round." She is always open to persuasion, and indeed she considers of great importance what the saleswoman tells her, even what her friends tell her. She will try on any number of things. Highest in her mind is the thought of finding something that everyone thinks suits her. Most women have an excellent sense of value when they buy clothes. They are always trying to find an unexpected bargain. Faced with a roomful of dresses, a woman may easily spend an hour going from one counter to another before selecting the dresses she wants to try on. It takes a great deal of time but gives great joy. Most dress shops supply chairs for the waiting husbands.

Passage Three

Two Dads Are Better than One

I've always envied people with only two parents. They never have to feel sorry for their real father because he is lonely, and they never have to feel they should care more about their stepfather because he is the one who has provided them with the necessities most of their lives. Since I have two fathers, I have known these feelings. I know what it is like trying to decide which father I should care about more so that I could tell my friends the next time they asked. It really should be a clear-cut decision. My two fathers are so different in everything that I should be able to look at these differences and decide whom ever to love more.

A major difference between the two is how responsible they are. My stepfather has always had a steady job. He enjoys going to work each day and knowing that at the end of the week he'll get a paycheck. With this paycheck he pays bills, buys groceries, and makes sure we all have clothes to wear. On the other hand, my father doesn't particularly care for steady jobs. He is a singer and has worked three or four nights a week in nightclubs most of his life. With his money, he buys things like new guitars and amplifiers. His idea of providing for us, as Mom tells me, is to send ten dollars a month, which is to be divided three ways. He only does this, however, when he's out of state.

Discipline is another major difference between my two fathers. My stepfather, who can be very strict at times, believes that children should obey their parents, do what they are told when they are told to do it, and respect their elders. My father, who was never disciplined himself, has quite different views. He has always encouraged my brothers and me to rebel against rules, to ask why we had to do certain things, and to resent being made to do things we thought were stupid (Going to bed at ten was stupid). My mother always told us that our father only did this to cause trouble, but I'm not so sure about that. Maybe she did, but then again maybe she thought going to bed at ten was stupid, too!

Education is another big issue my stepfather is concerned about. He believes, like many people, that to be able to succeed in life, one has to have a good education. He always told us that he didn't want us to turn out like he did, a truck driver who had to be away from his family for weeks at a time. He used to punish me and my brothers for making C's on our report cards. His theory is that a C is average, and his kids are not average. I wouldn't place any money on that. My father believes that an education is good to have, but one doesn't have to have it to survive. He always says, "Look at me; I made it." I don't think, however, that I would call sleeping in the back of a station wagon "making it."

So here I have it. All their differences down on paper, and I can look at them objectively and decide which father to love more, but it isn't that easy. I love my father because he is just that, my natural father. I respect him; I am obligated to him, and I want to make him proud of me. Then there is my stepfather, whom I respect very much; whom I feel obligated to; whom I want to make proud of me; and, most important of all, whom I have grown to love as much as any child could possibly love a parent. I guess I'll never really know which father I love more. I don't see why I should have to love either more. I think I'll just love both of them in almost equal amounts.

Unit Seven

Cause and Effect

Introductory Remarks

What are the causes of your breaking up with your girl or boyfriend? What are the causes of the growing divorce rate in China? What caused you to go to college? What caused the AIDS epidemic? What caused population migration from the countryside to the city in China?

What might be effects of China's peaceful rising? What might be effects of China's entry into WTO? What would be the effects if you failed to enter the university? What would be the effects if China abolished death penalty? What would be the effects if undergraduates in colleges and universities were to get married? What effects does university education have on your view of the world?

Attempting to answer the aforementioned questions, you will find that cause and effect papers are among the most common and the most fun papers in a composition course. We are engaged in cause-and-effect analysis regularly because it helps us make sense of the world, examine why an event or action occurred (the causes) or what resulted from the event or action (the effects), or both, and recall the past, understand the present, and predict the future.

The purpose of a cause-and-effect analysis is to inform, persuade or share. For example, you have written an essay explaining what causes leaves to change color and fall from the trees in autumn. Your examination of the cause surely informs your readers. Similarly, if you wrote an essay explaining what happens to teenagers when their parents divorce, your purpose could also be to inform your readers.

Often a cause-and-effect analysis serves to persuade a reader. For example, you could explain the effects of undergraduate marriage to persuade your reader not to get married during the four years of college education. Also, you could explain the effects of the legal recognition of same-sex marriage to persuade the government not to provide legal protection to civil partners.

Sometimes the writer of a cause-and-effect analysis wishes to share. If you wrote about how your breaking up with your girl friend or boy friend affected you, your purpose could be to share your feelings and experiences. Similarly, if you wrote about what caused you to make the decision of being single, your purpose might also be to share feelings and experiences.

Warm-Up Exercise：Reading and Discussion

Directions：Read the following cause and effect passages and discuss the writing skills in small groups.

Passage One

Subway Syndrome

Most people are unaware of the fact that a new ailment has developed among subway users. Called "subway syndrome," it causes people to turn pale and cold and even to faint. Commuters misdiagnose the symptoms—acute chest pains and disgust—and rush to hospital emergency rooms in the belief that they are about to die of a heart attack. Hearing that their heart attack is only a case of nerves makes them feel better.

What makes people get sick on subways? One is that they rush off to work in the morning without having eaten a proper breakfast. Sudden dizziness attacks them. A second cause is the overcrowding and following feeling of claustrophobia, which brings on stress and anxiety. In addition, they are so afraid of mechanical failure, fire, and crime that they show signs of panic—men by having chest pains and women by becoming hysterical. Contributing especially to their stress are other factors: overcrowding of both sexes, continual increase in the number of passengers, and people's inability to avoid interacting with strangers.

Noise, lack of space, summer heat, fear of entrapment underground—it is a wonder that more people don't have subway syndrome. What treating measures can a commuter take to protect himself or herself from the disease? Eat a good breakfast, concentrate on pleasant thoughts as you stand surrounded, bounce a bit on your toes, and roll your head. Thus, mind and body will be restored to an appearance of normality despite the adverse conditions of subway transportation.

Passage Two

The Wrong Examples

By David L. Evans

As a college admissions officer I am alarmed at the dearth of qualified black male candidates. Often in high schools that are 90 percent black, all the African American students who come to my presentation are female! This gender disparity persists to college matriculation where the black male population almost never equals that of the female.

What is happening to these young men? Who or what is influencing them? I submit that the absence of male role models and slanted television images of black males have something to do with it.

More than half of black children live in homes headed by women, and almost all of the black teachers they encounter are also women. This means that most African American male children do not often meet black male role models in their daily lives. They must look beyond their immediate surroundings for exemplary black men to emulate. Lacking in-the-flesh models, many look to TV for black heroes.

Unfortunately, TV images of black males are not particularly diverse. Their usual roles are to display physical prowess, sing, dance, play a musical instrument, or make an audience laugh. These roles are enticing and generously rewarded. But the reality is that success comes to only a few extraordinarily gifted performers or athletes.

A foreigner watching American TV would probably conclude that most successful black males are either athletes or entertainers. That image represents both success and failure.

Success, because the substantial presence of blacks in sports, music, and sitcoms is a milestone in the struggle beginning almost 50 years ago to penetrate the racial barriers of big-league athletics and television. It is a failure because the overwhelming success of a few highly visible athletes, musicians, and comedians has typecast black males. Millions see these televised roles as a definition of black men. Nowhere is this more misleading than in the inner city, where young males see it as "the way out."

Ask a random sample of Americans to identify Michael Jordan, Bo Jackson, Magic Johnson, Hammer, Prince, Eddie Murphy, or Mike Tyson. Correct responses would probably exceed 90 percent. Then ask them to identify Colin Powell, August Wilson, Franklin Thomas, Mike Espy, Walter Massey, Earl Graves, or the late Reginald Lewis and I doubt that 10 percent would respond correctly. The second group contains the chairman of the Joint Chiefs of Staff, a Pulitzer Prize-winning playwright, the president of the Ford Foundation, the secretary of agriculture, the director of the National Science Foundation, the publisher of *Black Enterprise* magazine, and the former CEO of a multimillion-dollar business.

The Democratic National Convention that nominated Bill Clinton [in 1992] brought Ron Brown, Jesse Jackson, David Dinkins, Kurt Schmoke, and Bernard Shaw into living rooms as impressive role models. Their relative numbers at the convention were in noticeable contrast to the black baseball players who made up nearly half of the All-Star teams on the Tuesday night of the convention.

This powerful medium has made the glamour of millionaire boxers, ballplayers, musicians, and comedians appear so close, so tangible that, to naive young boys, it seems only a dribble or dance step away. In the hot glare of such surrealism, schoolwork and prudent personal behavior can become irrelevant.

Impressionable young black males are not the only Americans getting this potent message. All TV viewers are subtly told that blacks are "natural" athletes, are "funny," and all of them have "rhythm." Such a thoroughly reinforced message doesn't lie dormant. A teacher who thinks every little black boy is a potential Bo Jackson or Eddie Murphy is likely to give his football practice a higher priority than his homework or to excuse his disruptive humor.

Section One: Introduction to Cause and Effect

What Is Cause and Effect?

Cause and effect refers to the method of development in which the writer analyzes the reason(s) for an action, event, or decision, or analyzes resulting consequences to support a point. Cause and effect essays seek to establish a casual relationship between two or more occurrences or facts. This type of academic evidence relies heavily upon logic and established evidence. In order to convince a discerning audience of your ideas, you must make them believe your chain of evidence. Thus, providing ample and supported evidence is a must.

Causes tell us what has led up to the particular subject being discussed:

- What caused you to enter college?
- What causes children to misbehave?
- What makes someone give up smoking?
- What causes globalization?

Effects tell us what has happened after the subject is discussed:

- The effects of urbanization
- The effects of smoking
- The effects of the failure of entering college
- The effects of divorce on teenage children

Types of Cause and Effect

Multiple Causes / Effects

This particular approach is used when the writer wants to emphasize that there are different causes creating a situation, or that different effects can, or will, rise out of a situation. An essay trying to explain the unprecedented upsurge of college students nationwide would reply on this approach to make it manifest that there are numerous factors causing the phenomenon.

Primary Cause / Effect

This approach to cause / effect is used when the writer understands that there are many different causes or effects, but certain ones hold more significance than the others. The writer will carefully select the causes or effects that have the most impact and then write an essay arguing for the importance of those particular choices. This particular approach requires specific explanation, usually with examples and data. The more the writer knows or has researched on the subject, the more effective this approach becomes.

Chain Cause / Effect

This form of cause / effect adopts a chronological approach to the subject. This approach recognizes that every effect becomes a cause for a new effect, and the new effect becomes the cause for another effect, and so on. For example:

Slowing economy causes lower tax receipts.

Lower tax receipts cause university budget cuts.

University budget cuts cause hiring freeze.

University hiring freeze causes classes to get cancelled.

Classes being cancelled cause you not to graduate.

The chain style of cause / effect essay picks up on these linked causes / effects, usually to show a remote cause or effect lurking yonder. If the writer wants to show long-term effects of oil spill on a coral reef or how losing the 1960 election caused Nixon to order the Watergate break-ins, he/she needs to use this method. Here the writer needs to deal with the process, but the focus is on the meaning and importance, not just the process itself.

Determine what the multiple causes and effects of the subject are. Then trace some of the more significant causes / effects out in chains. Determine which method of organization best fits the purpose / focus of the essay. Determine the best order to present the information: most important to least, least important to most, chronological order, from causes to effects, or effects to causes. The order should be what is necessary to best emphasize the purpose / focus / meaning of the overall essay. Be sure to have the necessary evidence / examples to back up the claims. Don't just tell the reader that a cause is important but try to prove it.

Section Two: Process of Writing Cause and Effect Papers

In a relatively short cause and effect essay, it is important to remember that it is not to cover both causes and effects. Actually, in a short essay of 150 to 250 words, it is important to write either "causes" or "effects," but not both. The reason for this is that it is simply not wise to try to cover too much information in a short essay.

Step One

State your organization. In all compositions, you should state your organization, which means that you should (1) tell your audience what you are going to tell them, (2) then tell them, and (3) then tell them what you told them.

Step Two

It is not necessary to list *all* of the causes or all of the effects in your essay, but before you begin to write your essay, list as many causes or effects as you can think of. For instance, if you want to write about the effects of air pollution in Guangzhou, you may start as follows:

Effects of Air Pollution in Guangzhou City
more sitting in front of the television
destruction of wildlife/necessity to stay indoors
decrease in tourism/negative world image
allergies
lower quality of life/headaches/running nose
shorter life span
poor visibility

Step Three

Support all causes or effects with supporting details. If you believe, for example, that an important effect of air pollution in Guangzhou is a lower quality of life for the city's residents, state your point clearly at the beginning of a paragraph and then provide supporting evidence to help your reader understand how or why that is true.

Step Four

Have a rationale for the order you present your information. There is often one major cause or effect that is the most important. Some recommend that you save your most important cause or effect to the end. By saving your most important cause or effect to the end, they say, you leave your reader with a very strong impression. Others say you should start with the most important cause or effect because that helps capture your reader's attention. In reality, there is no single best answer to the order of major causes or effects. Develop your own rationale for the order in which you present your information.

Step Five

Finally, maintain your focus. In a short cause or effect essay of 150 to 250 words, limit the range of your topic to either the *causes* or *effects* of something. A cause or effect essay doesn't recommend how to change the situation or give opinions about why the situation is good or bad. It simply examines the reasons or results of it.

Section Three: Structuring a Cause and Effect Composition

Focus: *Causes*

Introduction (thesis statement)

First cause

Second cause

Third cause

Final (and the most important) cause

Conclusion (restatement of your thesis or summary of your key points)

Focus: *Effects*

Introduction (thesis statement)

First effect

Second effect

Third effect

Final (and the most important) effect

Conclusion (restatement of your thesis or summary of your key points)

Focus: *Cause and Effect*

Introduction (thesis statement)

Causes

Effects

Conclusion (restatement of your thesis or summary of your key points)

The structure possibilities for cause and effect pattern:

The cause(s) comes first, then the effect(s).

The effect(s) comes first, then the cause(s).

The writer traces a complex causal chain.

An example for cause and effect composition organization:

Introduction tells about how the subject came up, gives the thesis statement, and names the audience who can benefit from knowing the information.

Body

A. Cause(s) or effect (s)

B. Effect(s) or cause (s)

C. Cause(s) and effect(s)

Conclusion

Section Four: Concrete Skills for Cause and Effect Composition

Step One

Choose a topic.

Step Two

Decide the focus of your topic. A cause-and-effect analysis can focus on causes or effects, or both.

    a. focus on causes (i. e. Identify some possible causes of the high divorce rate in the United States.)

b. focus on effects（i. e. Discuss the impact of the high divorce rate on children.）

c. focus on causes and effects（i. e. 1978 was a special year in China. Choose one social, political, or economic event that occurred during this year, analyze its causes, and briefly note how the event influenced later development of China.）

Step Three

Gather information on your topic. Each cause and effect should be considered as a generalization that must be supported with adequate details.

Step Four

Develop a thesis including introduction of key points. Approaches to the introduction include explaning why an understanding of the cause-and-effect relationship is important and introducing briefly causes of your subject if the essay will discuss effects, and vice versa.

Step Five

Arrange your evidence in a progressive order, chronological order, or categorical order.

Step Six

Develop a conclusion. A cause-and-effect analysis can conclude in a number of ways, including drawing a conclusion from the cause-and-effect relationship and summarizing the key points, if the causes and / or effects are complex.

Mini-task One: *Writing Practice*

Directions：Select ONE of the following issues and write a cause-and-effect essay in about 200 words. In writing the essay, you must first decide what you are going to focus on：the causes, the effects or both.

1. My favorite tourist attraction
2. My favorite sport
3. My favorite film star
4. My sparetime interest
5. The changes of weddings in recent years in China
6. The development of auto industry in China

Mini-task Two: *Reading and Discussion*

Directions：Read and discuss your writing in sharing groups.

Homework

Task One: Writing

Directions: Write a cause and / or effect composition on one of the following topics in about 200 words.

1. Think back to your earlier school days and recall a happy event. Write an essay that analyzes the causes and / or effects of this event.
2. Analyze the effects of some recent innovation or invention such as the Camcorder, cell phone, video games, or iphone.
3. Analyze the causes and effects of a long-term friendship you have had.
4. Identify a problem on your campus (inadequate housing, high tuition, isolation, etc.), and analyze its causes and / or effects.
5. Explain the effects attending college has had on your life.
6. Explain why some high school students drop out of school in the countryside in China.
7. Explain the long-term effects of a childhood experience.
8. If you or a family member has been laid off, explain its effects on your family.
9. Explain how someone other than a family member has influenced your life.
10. Where we grow up has an enormous effect on whom and what we become. How did the place where you grew up (big city, small town, remote village, poor neighborhood, etc.) affect you?

Task Two: Reading

Directions: Read the following cause-and-effect passages and summarize the writing skills used in each passage respectively. You are also expected to provide comments on the valuable points as well as the points you think should be improved regarding the writing skills.

Passage One

The Effects of Living in a Foreign Country

Living away from your country can be a really interesting and unforgettable experience, but at the same time it has very important effects on one's life. The purpose of this essay is to discuss the three main effects that living in another country can produce in your personal life.

The major effect, and also a very common one, is that once you start a regular life away from home, you miss everything. This fact doesn't mean that you are unhappy but that you are aware of being on your own. Missing your family and the attention they all paid to you is common to all. Little details like sitting on a Sunday morning watching TV alone instead of helping your dad organizing his things or having a nice chat with your mom make you realize how valuable your family really is. It is also completely acceptable to miss all the facilities you used to have back at home, like your house, your car, your bed, and your bathroom. It is obvious then that you have started to appreciate everything you had back where you belong.

The second main effect would be learning how to accept another type of society and culture into your daily life. Since you are living in a place with different customs and traditions from yours, you have to be able to develop yourself in unknown conditions. This means making new friends, learning other points of view, accepting different opinions and values, and seizing every opportunity you have to go to new places. Therefore, you'll be able to achieve true knowledge. Suggesting to change your mind totally or to be square minded would be foolish; the best thing to do would be to stick to your most important values and, accordingly, change those that you believe could be improved.

The most significant effect of living away from home is the independent behavior that grows inside of you. Living on your own far from your family gives you a lot of experiences toward organizing your life. Since it is up to you to clean your room, wash your clothes, and organize your expenses, it is predictable that you will develop a good and strong sense of responsibility. Being independent and responsible will help you get through life every goal you want to achieve.

Living far from home, even for a short period of time, can be really hard at the beginning. We have to remember that all changes are difficult, but they are necessary to go through to build character. Most important of all, it helps us appreciate everything we have.

Not realizing how lucky we are can be a really bad mistake because things don't last forever and we have to make the best out of them.

Passage Two

The Effects of Cigarette Smoking

There have been numerous campaigns against cigarette smoking communicating that smoking causes death. But a threat to health doesn't seem to be a good reason for quitting anymore. People somehow block themselves and ignore all the information that is given to them. The purpose of this essay is to discuss three effects of cigarette smoking, besides the broadly mentioned possibility of developing cancer or dying, which are the smell of smoke, the stained teeth, and the cost of doing it.

The first effect of cigarette smoking, and probably the one that the non-smokers hate the most, is that it permeates everything around it. Smokers usually have smelly hair, breath, clothes, and, if they smoke indoors, a smelly room. The stench of cigarette smoke is very penetrating and hard to remove. Even if the person quits smoking the odor remains for a long time.

The second effect of cigarette smoking is one that most people don't even take into consideration. It stains the teeth yellow or sometimes even brown. Since this effect is long term, most people are not aware of it when they begin smoking. The truth is that a cigarette stain is very hard to eliminate from the teeth, and it will probably cost a considerable amount of money if you want to clean the stain. Yellow teeth are disgusting because they give an unhygienic image and make people look older.

The third effect of smoking is that it will eventually end up affecting the smoker's personal finance. Depending on the country the prices of cigarettes can differ. But even at an affordable price the regular consumption of cigarettes will eventually take its economic toll.

These are only three out of many other effects that cigarette smoking can have, but to any sensible person they are more than enough to realize that smoking is bad. People can possibly be proud of calling themselves smokers. It is terrible for health as well as personal appearance. In the end, those who live in poverty, stink of smoke, and have yellow teeth are the people who are affected the most by this life threatening activity.

Passage Three

I Want a Wife

By Judy Brady

I belong to that classification of people known as wives. I am a Wife. And, not altogether incidentally, I am a mother.

Not too long ago a male friend of mine appeared on the scene fresh from a recent divorce. He had one child, who is, of course, with his ex-wife. He is looking for another wife. As I thought about him while I was ironing one evening, it suddenly occurred to me that I, too, would like to have a wife. Why do I want a wife?

I would like to go back to school so that I can become economically independent, support myself, and if need be, support those dependent upon me. I want a wife who will work and send me to school. And while I am going to school I want a wife to take care of my children. I want a wife to keep track of the children's doctor and dentist appointments, and to keep track of mine, too. I want a wife who will wash the children's clothes and keep them mended. I want a wife who is a good nurturant attendant to my children, who arranges for their schooling, makes sure that they have an adequate social life with their peers, takes them to the park, the zoo, etc. I want a wife who takes care of the children when they are sick, a wife who arranges to be around when the children need special care, because, of course, I cannot miss classes at school. My wife must arrange to lose time at work and not lose the job. It may mean a small cut in my wife's income from time to time, but I guess I can tolerate that. Needless to say, my wife will arrange and pay for the care of the children while my wife is working.

I want a wife who will take care of my physical needs. I want a wife who will keep my house clean. A wife who will pick up after my children, a wife who will pick up after me. I want a wife who will keep my clothes clean, ironed, mended, replaced when need be, and who will see to it that my personal things are kept in their proper place so that I can find what I need the minute I need it. I want a wife who cooks the meals, a wife who is a good cook. I want a wife who will plan the menus, do the necessary grocery shopping, prepare the meals, serve them pleasantly, and then do the cleaning up while I do my studying. I want a wife who will care for me when I am sick and sympathize with my pain and loss of time from school. I want a wife to go along when our family takes a vacation so that someone can continue to care for me and my children when I need a rest and change of scene.

I want a wife who will not bother me with rambling complaints about a wife's duties.

But I want a wife who will listen to me when I feel the need to explain a rather difficult point I have come across in my course of studies. And I want a wife who will type my papers for me when I have written them.

I want a wife who will take care of the details of my social life. When my wife and I are invited out by my friends, I want a wife who will take care of the babysitting arrangements. When I meet people at school I want a wife who will have the house clean, will prepare a special meal, serve it to me and my friends, and not interrupt when I talk about things that interest me and my friends. I want a wife who will have arranged that the children are fed and ready for bed before my guests arrive so that the children do not bother us. I want a wife who takes care of the needs of my guests so that they feel comfortable, who makes sure that they have an ashtray, that they are offered a second helping of the food, that their wine glasses are replenished when necessary, that their coffee is served to them as they like it. And I want a wife who knows that sometimes I need a night out by myself.

I want a wife who is sensitive to my sexual needs, a wife who makes love passionately and eagerly when I feel like it, a wife who makes sure that I am satisfied. And, of course, I want a wife who will not demand sexual attention when I am not in the mood for it. I want a wife who assumes the complete responsibility for birth control, because I do not want more children. I want a wife who will remain sexually faithful to me so that I do not have to clutter up my intellectual life with jealousies. And I want a wife who understands that my sexual needs may entail more than strict adherence to monogamy. I must, after all, be able to relate to people as fully as possible.

If, by chance, I find another person more suitable as a wife than the wife I already have, I have the liberty to replace my present wife with another one. Naturally, I will expect a fresh, new life; my wife will take the children and be solely responsible for them so that I am left free.

When I am through with school and have a job, I want my wife to quit working and remain at home so that my wife can more fully and completely take care of a wife's duties.

My God, who wouldn't want a wife?

Unit Eight

Classification and Division

第八单元　归纳分类法

要点提示："物以类聚、人以群分。"以适当的逻辑方法对人、事、物或信息予以归纳或分类可以提高获取信息的速度,提升认知效率。归纳是将具有相同属性的人、事、物按照特定原则归入同一类别,而分类则是将具有相同属性的人、事、物依据特定原则细分为更小的类别。二者相辅相成,共同达成分解人、事、物之目的,从而帮助我们更好地理解人、事和物。归纳分类写作的核心是原则适用的逻辑合理性,主旨阐释的明确性,以及归入或分出因由论证的充分性。

Introductory Remarks

Classification is a method of ordering information. It is a systematic grouping of elements into different categories according to certain logical principle. Just as comparison and contrast, cause and effect, classification and division is also a common and interesting type of composition. For example, in colleges and universities, books in a library are shelved according to subjects; in the job market, job vacancies are listed in accordance with professions such as marketing, business management, human resource management, administration, and financial services. TV Guide lists programs according to the day of the week and time of day; and instructors can be classified into positive, neutral, and negative according to their attitudes to teaching.

Without classification, learning and gaining access to information would be enormously difficult and time-consuming. Without the principles of organization that classification supplies, we would not know where to look for the information we need and we would have trouble seeing how items relate to each other. To understand this, imagine a library without a classification system. If you wanted to read a mystery, but you had no author or title in mind, you would have to scan the shelves until you got lucky and ran across an appropriate book. Fortunately, libraries have classification systems that allow you to go quickly right to the right place where all the mysteries are shelved.

Warm-Up Exercise: *Reading and Response*

Directions: Read the passages given below and provide comments on the valuable points as well as the points you think should be improved.

Passage One

Let the Reader Beware

American young women cannot help feeling pressed to be attractive, glamorous, and sexy. Many popular fashion magazines such as *Glamour*, *Seventeen*, *Mademoiselle*, *Teen*, *Vogue*, and *Harper's Bazaar* portray how the ideal woman should look. Marlo Thomas, Cher, Ellen Burstyn, Cybill Shepherd, Princess Caroline of Monaco, and even Susan Ford model in these magazines.

But can the average American girl really profit by identifying with these people? The only helpful fashion advice is practical. Since most American girls are neither rich nor gifted with perfect figures and flawless complexions, most fashion magazines are not very helpful to the average American girl.

With today's inflation, the career girl and the college girl need very practical fashion advice. Both require a variety of clothes that are stylish and reasonably priced. The most recent issue of *Glamour* features outfits consisting of midi skirts or pants, woolen sweaters, patterned shirts, and crazy-colored argyle knee socks. These outfits are incomplete without such accessories as head-hugging hats, scarves, skinny belts, bangles, earrings, gold necklaces, mod watches, and leather bags. Each outfit, excluding the accessories, costs a staggering figure, considering the variety of clothes necessary for work or school. Evening dresses also come with a high price tag. One issue of *Seventeen* features Susan Ford in formal dresses, the latest spring prom look. What those dresses cost hardly seems worth it for one night.

Some of the expensive clothes are faddish. In two years the hemline has gone from mini to maxi. *Mademoiselle* says that yesterday's classic blazer is being replaced by big bulky sweaters, and platform shoes are giving way to cowboy boots. Some outfits are appropriate for special occasions only—like the bizarre outfit *Seventeen* advised for a wine-tasting party. Today's girl needs reasonable, comfortable, attractive clothing for school, work, and recreation, and these are scarce in the popular fashion magazines.

In addition, the clothes shown are designed for a tall, pencil-thin figure. When one considers how unaverage that kind of figure is, then adds in the fact of plastic surgery—as when Cher had her breasts redesigned and her buttocks lifted, and compounds all of that with the magic thrills a camera can perform, she has to wonder what one has to be to wear these clothes well.

The American girl needs advice on how to select clothes that are comfortable, flattering, and affordable. In the popular fashion magazines, she is instead advised to buy clothes that are expensive, faddish, and unbecoming to the average figure. Let the reader—and the buyer—beware.

Passage Two

Motor Vehicles

Vehicles are used for a variety of purposes. Considering those purposes can help one make a good purchase. When drivers are considering the purchase of an automobile, they might consider the vast array of vehicles in the market. Vehicles can be categorized using three basic approaches: those for personal use, those for recreation, and those for work. Automobiles used for personal use are those that are typically efficient at using gasoline and minimizing the amount of emissions released in the environment. People often use these for going to work or doing chores. Americans typically enjoy driving Hondas, Buiks, Toyotas, Chevrolets, Dodges and the like, all of which make various models for passenger transportation. These cars usually seat between four to six people and are designed to carry occupants from work to home and back—whether the distance is a long commute or a short one.

Automobiles that are used for pleasure—sometimes for pleasure and not for work—include Miatas, Blazers and Campers. Miatas are small two-seater cars that can be convertible. Miatas and Blazers are sporty. Blazers, however, are larger, and can be used to store camping equipment. Blazers are considered SUVs (sports utility vehicle). Young people and families are attracted to Blazers because they can be used for recreation and for transportation to and from work. Campers are much larger than Blazers. Such vehicles make it possible for families to take vacations and live temporarily in the vehicle. Some come equipped with everything the users will need: showers, small toilets, kitchens and the like.

A third category of vehicle is used strictly for work on the farm, in construction work and for transporting large amounts of goods. In the United States, we call this type of vehicle a truck. The truck comes in several sizes and can have multiple uses. A long-bed full-size pickup truck or small-bed half-ton truck can be used by people who own small construction businesses or by those who run small and large farms. Commercial tractor trailers or semi trucks are used by businesses usually to transport large amounts of goods across long distances to people who live in various areas of the United States.

All of these types of vehicles can be used in other areas of course. The person who is considering the purchase of a vehicle should consider carefully what the vehicle is going to be used for before making the purchase. Most people in the U. S. are somewhat informed about the types of vehicles available for purchase as advertisers provide information about uses in advertisements. Such advertisements can be found in newspapers, on television, and on the radio. Another excellent source of information for the purchase of a vehicle is "*Consumer's Report*" available in magazine form or on the Internet. Purchasing a vehicle takes a little research, but it is well worth the effort. It is wise to do research before making a purchase.

Section One: Definition of Classification and Division

Classification is a process of sorting people, things, or ideas into groups or categories to help make them more understandable. The classification essay categorizes a subject, moving from specific examples to groups that share common characteristics. *Examples* might include: levels of skills—paperboy, waitress, plumber, lawyer, brain surgeon, athletes, actors, singers, chefs, and so on and so forth.

Division is similar to classification, but instead of grouping numerous items into categories, division begins with one item and breaks it down into parts. The division essay separates a single concept into its subunits or a whole into its parts. *Examples* of this might include dividing a college into its departments (biology, philosophy, music, etc.), a city into neighborhoods, or television shows into news, features, sports, weather, and editorials.

Classification groups and division divides ideas according to one principle. Classification uses categories and division uses parts that are exclusive and comprehensive. Classification or division fully explains each category or part.

Mini-task: *Reading and Discussion*

Directions: Read the following introductory paragraphs of classification and work out the principles of classification in small groups.

Paragraph One

Classification of Restaurant Customers

"I've been here for ten minutes and my server hasn't taken my order yet!" This is a direct quote from me before I worked at a restaurant. I never looked to see how many tables my server actually had or how much running I made them do. The sad truth is most people do not notice these details either, which may affect the tip their server will receive. By looking at the attitude and maintenance of restaurant customers, you can classify them into three categories according to their tipping patterns: the "'hmm... how good were they?' tippers," the "stick-to-the-fifteen-percent tippers," and the "I-am-or-once-was-a-server tippers."

Paragraph Two

Classification of Friends

Ever since I was a child, my mother raised me to recognize and appreciate various kinds of friends. There are three different kinds of friends in my life. I classify them according to how well I know them and how well they know me. We encounter each of them every day, whether in school, home, or at the gym. However, we rarely spend much time actually thinking about and classifying these people. First, there are the "pest friends"—general acquaintances. Next, there are "guest friends"—social partners. Lastly, we have "best friends"—our true friends.

Paragraph Three

Classification of Businesses

Classification of Businesses according to their types of activity: Primary Sector Businesses: The gathering of raw materials, such as fish, oil, or coal from the sea or land, using the earth to grow things such as crops or trees. Examples: Rio Tinto (mining), JCI Gold (mining), Anglo Amer (mining), BP (oil and gas), and Soco International (oil and gas）. Secondary Sector Businesses：The processing of raw materials into finished goods. Examples of this are food production, computer component manufacture, and car manufacture. Examples：Schweppes（food and drink）, Unilever（food and drink）, Intel（computer component production）, and Ati（computer component production）. Tertiary Sector Businesses：This sector contains organizations supplying services, and includes both commercial services providers（banking, finance, and retail）, as well as direct service providers（health and education）. Examples：Stagecoach（transport）, Air China（transport）, CGNU（insurance）, BT（telecommunications）and Natwest（banking）.

Paragraph Four

Classification of Television

Television can be divided into two categories determined by its means of transmission. First, there is broadcast television, which reaches the masses through broad-based airwave transmission of television signals. Second, there is nonbroadcast television, which provides for the needs of individuals or specific interest groups through controlled transmission techniques.

Section Two: Purposes of Classification and Division

Sorting

Sorting is when the writer takes a large group of things（the larger the better）, like the members of a class, or the students in a school, or the shoppers at a hardware store, and divides them into smaller groups. The writer should focus on what separates the group from the main population, and connect the subjects to each other.

Sorting can be done on many levels. It can be as broad or precise as the writer needs it to be. Generally, the more the writer knows about the subject, the more precise it can be. To the average person, a beetle is just a bug. They recognize that it is not a mosquito or dragonfly, but that is almost about it all. But to an expert on beetles, there are scarab beetles, stag beetles and longhorn beetles. The differences are very important to the experts, and if they choose to write about those differences, they need to make sure that the reader sees and understands that importance. This leads us to the second step：explaining.

Explaining

Explaining is the real core of the classification/division essay. Sorting and organizing things into groups is easy. Small children regularly sort their crayons (the reds here, the blues there, etc.) Almost everything that we encounter has been organized/sorted in some way. Imagine going to the grocery store with the groceries placed on the shelves alphabetically, or in random fashion. That would be quite a scene shocking to everyone! The grocery store works because we know where things are supposed to be, in general. However, did you ever ask why certain parts of a grocery store are regularly placed in the back corners? Almost every grocery store will place the meat and dairy in back corners deliberately so that the shopper has to walk past all the other groceries in order to make their basic purchases. That's the explaination of the organization. See, there's a meaning or a purpose to the groupings and / or placing.

Most writers will use labels for their categories. If they are describing standard categories (like types of beetles), they will use the standard categories. Then the explanation will be about what the content of the standard categories can tell us. If they are writing a division based more on their own experiences and knowledge (types of grocery shoppers), then the labels will be more unique and individual. Thus, the meaning is often related to the reasons that one particular category exists, not how many items are in it.

Section Three: Structure of Classification and Division Essay

Classification Structure:

Paragraph One: Introduction
- Thesis Statement

Paragraph Two: Body
- Identifies, in separate paragraphs, the various categories with examples.

Paragraph Three: Conclusion
- Restates the categories of the thesis and, as a significance—or answer to the question "so what?" implied in any composition, stresses the value of this classification system.

Division Structure:

Paragraph One: Introduction

- Thesis statement (idea or object to be analyzed, and to what end)

Paragraph Two: Body

- Renders the parts, in separate paragraphs, with examples and transitional materials to provide a sense of inter-relatedness.

Paragraph Three: Conclusion

- Restates the parts of the thesis and attempts a synthesis or new understanding of the constituent parts.

Mini-task One: *Writing*

Directions: Write a short classification / division-based essay of about 150 words by dividing and classifying the kinds of jobs university students usually have. Organize your composition with an introduction, body, and conclusion.

Mini-task Two: *Reading and Discussion*

Directions: Read the following essay of classification and division by a student, which has strengths and weaknesses. Read it carefully, and answer the evaluation questions given below.

Evaluation Questions:

1. Are the elements grouped according to certain logical principle of classification?
2. What purpose does the classification serve?
3. Is it clear about the elements in each grouping?
4. Are all points adequately developed?
5. Are all points relevant to the thesis and topic sentences?
6. Is there any overlapping in the development of the body?
7. Are the comparable points discussed in each section of the essay?
8. Are signal devices used to connect various parts of the essay?

Reading Passage

Good Friends

I am fortunate. Over the past few years, I have had a number of good friends. Some of them I would trust with my life; the rest of them I couldn't even trust to cross the street by themselves. Although very different, my good friends fall into two groups.

In the first group are the intellectuals. I enjoy being with these people because I can have intelligent conversations with them. Last fall during the presidential campaign, they were the only friends I had that I could discuss the election with—without having to explain who George Bush is. When I get together with these friends, we talk about our classes, argue about issues, and trade ideas. I feel mentally stimulated by these friends. My intellectual friends and I also help each other with classes. Kirk helps me with computers. Audra helps me with chemistry. Laura helps me with English. I help them with jogging class.

My second group of friends is vastly different from the intellectuals. These are the jocks. With this group of friends, I share the most: a love for sport, the need to complete, and an understanding of the pain, dedication, frustration, and exhilaration, the athlete experiences. The jocks are my most loyal friends, the ones I can count on to be there when I need to be straightened out. One friend, in particular, has been there for me. Wess has been a good friend since we started playing basketball together in sixth grade. We spend hours together each day working out, shooting hoops, and just hanging out. Two years ago when I was recovering from a knee injury, Wess would not let me quit no matter how frustrated I got. He sat with me during therapy, forced me to exercise until I got back in shape, and refused to let me back down from the challenge, even when I insisted I was going to quit.

If the quality of a person's life can be measured by the friends he or she has, then I am one lucky guy. Whether intellectuals or jocks, my friends are the best.

Homework

Task One: Writing Practice

Directions: Write a classification and / or division composition in around 200 words on one of the topics given below. You need to work out a proper title of your own that gives your composition a direction.

1. Types of cars in China.
2. Types of your friends.
3. Types of pastimes university students enjoy.

4. Classify the type of classmates you study with based on their personalities.

5. Categorize human personalities by the kind of cars people drive.

6. Categorize the books you read.

7. Classify university instructors in China.

Task Two: Reading

Directions: Read the following classification and division essays. Each has strengths and aspects that could be improved. Read them carefully, and answer the evaluation questions given below.

Evaluation Questions:

1. Are the elements grouped according to certain logical principle of classification?

2. What purpose does the classification serve?

3. Is it clear about the elements in each grouping?

4. Are all points adequately developed?

5. Are all points relevant to the thesis and topic sentences?

6. Is there a clear thesis, either stated or strongly implied?

7. Does the classification have an introduction? If so, is it appropriate and interest-holding? If there is no introduction, should there be?

8. Is there a formal conclusion? If not, should there be one? If there is a conclusion, does it bring the essay to a satisfying close?

9. In general, is the word choice specific, economical, and simple? What words, if any, would you like to replace with more proper ones?

10. Does the essay flow well because of adequate sentence variety? If not, where is sentence variety needed?

Passage One

Economic Systems

There are various ways in which individual economic units can interact with one another. Three basic ways may be described as the market system, the administered system, and the traditional system.

In a market system, individual economic units are free to interact with each other in the marketplace. It is possible to buy commodities from other economic units or sell commodities to them. In a market, transactions may take place via barter or money exchange. In a barter economy, real goods such as automobiles, shoes, and pizzas are traded against each other. Obviously, finding somebody who wants to trade my old car in exchange for a sailboat may not always be an easy task. Hence, the introduction of money as a medium of exchange eases transactions considerably. In the modern market economy, goods and services are bought or sold for money.

An alternative to the market system is administrative control by some agency over all transactions. This agency will issue edicts or commands as to how much of each kind of goods and services should be produced, exchanged, and consumed by each economic unit. Central planning may be one way of administering such an economy. The central plan, drawn up by government, shows amounts of each commodity produced by the various firms and allocated to different households for consumption.

In a traditional society, production and consumption patterns are governed by tradition: every person's place within the economic system is fixed by parentage, religion, and custom. Transactions take place on the basis of tradition, too. People belonging to a certain group of caste may have an obligation to care for other persons, provide them with food and shelter, care for their health, and provide for their education. Clearly, in a system where every decision is made on the basis of tradition alone, progress may be difficult to achieve, and a stagnant society may result.

Passage Two

Three Passions I have

Three passions, simple but overwhelmingly strong, have governed my life: the longing for love, the search for knowledge, and unbearable pity for the suffering of mankind. These passions, like great winds, have blown me hither and thither, in a wayward course over a deep ocean of anguish, reaching to the very verge of despair.

I have sought love, first, because it brings ecstasy—ecstasy so great that I would often have sacrificed all the rest of my life for a few hours for this joy. I have sought it, next, because it relieves loneliness—that terrible loneliness in which one shivering consciousness looks over the rim of the world into the cold unfathomable lifeless abyss. I have sought it, finally, because in the union of love I have seen, in a mystic miniature, the prefiguring vision of the heaven that saints and poets have imagined. This is what I sought, and though it might seem too good for human life, this is what—at last—I have found.

With equal passion I have sought knowledge. I have wished to understand the hearts of men. I have wished to know why the stars shine. A little of this, but not much, I have achieved.

Love and knowledge, so far as they were possible, led me upward toward the heavens. But always pity brought me back to earth. Echoes of cries of pain reverberate in my heart. Children in famine, victims tortured by oppressors, helpless old people a burden to their sons, and the whole world of loneliness, poverty, and pain make a mockery of what human life should be. I long to alleviate the evil, but I cannot, and I too suffer.

This has been my life. I have found it worth living, and would gladly live it again if the chance were offered me.

Passage Three

Money

Aristotle, the Greek philosopher, summed up the four chief qualities of money some 2,000 years ago. It must be lasting and easy to recognize, to divide, and to carry about. In other words it must be "durable, distinct, divisible and portable." When we think of money today, we picture it as round, flat pieces of metal which we call coins, or as printed paper notes. But there are still parts of the world today where coins and notes are of no use. They will buy nothing, and a traveler might starve if he had none of the particular local "money" to exchange for food.

Among isolated people who are not often reached by traders from outside, commerce usually means barter. There is a direct exchange of goods. Perhaps it is fish for vegetables, or meat for grain. For this kind of simple trading, money is not needed, but there is often something that everyone wants and everybody can use, such as salt, shells, or iron and copper. These things—salt, shells or metals—are still used as money in out-of-the-way parts of the world today.

Salt may rather be a strange substance to use as money, but in countries where the food of the people is mainly vegetable, it is often an absolute necessity. Cakes of salt, stamped to show their value, were used as money in some places until recent times, and cakes of salt will still buy goods in Borneo and parts of Africa.

Cowrie sea shells have been used as money at some time or another over the greater part of the Old World. These were collected mainly from the beaches of the Maldives Islands in the Indian Ocean, and were traded to India and China. In Africa, cowries were traded right across the continent from East to West. Four or five thousand went for one Maria Theresa dollar. An Austrian silver coin was once accepted as money in many parts of Africa.

Metal, valued by weight, were early coins in many parts of the world. Iron, in lumps, bars or rings, is still used in many countries instead of money. It can either be exchanged for goods, or made into tools or weapons. The early money of China, apart from shells, was of bronze, made in flat, round pieces with a hole in the middle, called "cash." The earliest of these are between three thousand and four thousand years old—older than the earliest coins of the eastern Mediterranean.

Nowadays, coins and notes have taken place of nearly all the more interesting forms of money, and although in one or two of the more remote countries people still hold it for future use on ceremonial occasions such as weddings and funerals, examples of early money will soon be found only in museums.

Unit Nine

Narration

第九单元　叙　事　法

要点提示："以人为鉴,可以明得失";"以己为鉴,可以知进取"。讲述切身经历,叙说心路历程是作者表达自我、认识自我的有效途径,亦是读者明得失、晓事理、获启迪的捷径。故事有时间、有地点、有人物、有起始、有发展、有结局,但这还不足以吸引读者。好的故事应当取材巧妙、寓意深刻、逻辑严密,应当精彩纷呈、高潮迭现、扣人心弦。好的故事给予读者的不只是阅读过程中的感受,更重要的是读后的感想。

Introductory Remarks

Narrative writing tells a story, which offers writers a chance to think and write about themselves, to explain how their experiences lead to some important realization or conclusion about their lives or about the world in general.

Narrative writing has a plot, a setting (where and when the story happens), and characters who have motives (reasons) for what they do. Good narrative writing is more than a list of random events. It has tension—a problem to be solved or a challenge to be overcome. There is a point to the story.

When you write a narrative essay, you are telling a story: an experience or event from his/her or your past; a recent or an ongoing experience or event; something that happened to you or somebody else.

When you tell a story, you are expected to include all the conventions of storytelling: plot, character, setting, climax, and ending. And you must bear in mind that the narrative essay is told from a particular point of view; it makes and supports a point; it is filled with precise detail; it uses vivid verbs and modifiers; and it uses conflict and sequence as does any story.

A narrative paragraph can also be an effective and interesting way to integrate significant background information into a variety of different essay types. Even if the essay as a whole primarily uses another method of development, the narrative paragraph can be incorporated into an essay to support a topic sentence in a particular paragraph and to call for ethical appeal at the same time. For example, you can tell one of your personal experiences as evidence to support the significance of fair process, or to support the statement of "Laws cannot change social values." Such narrative additions can help you as a writer create ethical appeal with your audience: the readers often look at such personal narrative favorably, seeing them as a touch of "realism" in an otherwise dry, esoteric, or abstract discussion.

Warm-Up Exercise: *Reading and Discussion*

Directions: Read the passage given below and discuss in small group the writing styles (the incident, the details, the choice of verbs, the point of view, the plot, the climax, the ending, etc.).

The Aria, an Italian Restaurant

By Nick Hansinger

My fiancée and I were out to dinner with two of her friends one weekend night. There was a long wait, but we were in no hurry, so we were happy to sit at the bar for a while and have a few drinks. We had some laughs with the bartender, and it came up in conversation that my fiancée sang opera. She has a gorgeous voice. I mean, you would think an angel had come to earth just to sing for you. Anyway, as we were joking around, the bartender offered us a round of drinks if she would sing an aria for the whole restaurant (it was, after all, an Italian restaurant and I suppose they thought it might be a real novelty to have an actual opera singer there). She politely declined.

Later on we had eaten our dinner, finished our desserts and were contemplating after dinner drinks when the bartender happened by and renewed his offer. In an instant my fiancée had grabbed my hand, and put me in a chair in the middle of the room. She began to sing and all I could do was to look at her in awe. The restaurant quickly fell silent. Everyone stopped talking; the waitresses and bus boys had stopped hustling about; the TV in the bar had suddenly been muted, and there was just this gorgeous, pure voice ringing through the entire place. For a moment I was aware of everyone looking at us, but it was only for a moment. I stared at her as she sang to me, and everyone and everything else disappeared. It was one of those moments, and one of those feelings that I simply can't describe, and won't ever forget. She finished the song, and everyone applauded, some yelling "Encore, encore!!" So she sang another song, not just to me this time, but also to the entire congregation. It was beautiful. Utterly gorgeous. Again she was received with great applause.

We went back to our seats, the bartender brought another round, and the restaurant went back to its former state of jingling glasses, clanking plates, and quiet, yet consistent rumble of 100 different conversations all happening at the same time. About five minutes later a lady and her husband came up to the table and introduced themselves. I don't remember their names, but I won't ever forget what happened next. She told my fiancée how beautiful she sounded and made a little light conversation asking about her career plans and what-not. Then, out of the blue she started telling us about her son who had been killed in a car crash not too long ago, and how much she missed him. She said that she had prayed to God every day and every night for a sign from him, and how when my fiancée started singing, she thought she sounded just like an angel, and that must be the sign. I asked the lady what her son's name was. When she told me, my heart nearly jumped out of my chest. She said his name was Nicholas. Without thinking, I stood up, offered her my hand and introduced myself. I said "My name is Nicholas, and everything is going to be O. K. " The lady's eyes welled up with tears while her husband stood behind her with an entirely blank look on his face. It was all I could do to keep from bursting into tears.

It's probably been a year and a half or two years since that night, and I still get tears in my eyes when I think about it. I'm not sure how I feel about that night, but I do know that it changed my life, and that I will never forget it. I've always believed in God, but I had never felt a presence like I did that night, even if only for a very brief moment. Despite that occurrence I still struggle with my faith. I guess I still have some things to work out in myself before I really come to grips with it. My fiancée and I are no longer together. We split up a few months after that night in the restaurant. Despite all the feelings we shared, it simply wasn't enough to keep us together. It takes more than love to make a relationship work. I don't hope for it to work between us anymore. I just accept what is, and what is not. I just try to enjoy the days as they come. I hope that she's doing the same.

Section One: Introduction to Narration

Principles

Once an incident is chosen, the writer should keep three principles in mind.

Make it interesting. Remember to involve readers in the story. It is much more interesting to actually recreate an incident for readers than to simply tell about it.

Find a generalization which the story supports. This is the only way the writer's personal experience will take on meaning for readers. This generalization does not have to encompass humanity as a whole; it can concern the writer, men, women, or children of various ages and backgrounds.

Work on details. Remember that although the main component of a narrative is the story, details must be carefully selected to support, explain, and enhance the story.

Conventions

In writing your narrative essay, keep the following principles in mind.

Narrations are generally written in the first person. However, the third person (*he*, *she*, or *it*) can also be used. Which person you use most often depends on whose perspective is being captured in the narration.

Narrations rely on concrete, specific details to make their point. These details should create a unified, dominant impression.

Narrations, as stories, should include these story elements: a plot (telling your readers what is happening), setting and characters; a climax (a peak experience often leading to the thesis, the important realization); and an ending (explaining how the incident resolved itself).

Features

The story should have an introduction that clearly indicates what kind of narrative essay it is (an event or a recurring activity, a personal experience, or an observation), and it should have a conclusion that makes a point.

The essay should include anecdotes. The author should describe the person, the scene, or the event in detail.

The occasion or person described must be suggestive in that your description and thoughts lead the reader to reflect on man's experience.

The point of view in narrative essays is usually first person. The use of "I" engages your readers in an intimate communication.

The writing in your essay should be lively and show some style. Try to describe ideas and events in new and different ways. Avoid using clichés. Again, write the basic ideas down, get it organized, and in your final editing process, work on wording.

Section Two: Structure of Narrative Writing

The Beginning

Begin with a "grabber" to hook your reader.

Describe scene.

Introduce characters.

The Development

Develop story with at least one specific incident or happening.

Keep your happenings in the correct order for time.

Include descriptions.

Here is where your action takes place.

A conversation might work well here.

This is a good place for a simile or two or even a bit of humor.

The Ending

Bring the story to a close, referring to events in the story for continuity.

Wrap it up with a satisfying ending, a zinger, or a humorous comment to leave your reader with a feeling of completion.

Mini-task: *Reading and Writing*

Directions: Read the passage given below and summarize the beginning, the development and the ending in around 150 words.

The Story of an Hour

By Kate Chopin

Knowing that Mrs. Mallard was afflicted with a heart trouble, great care was taken to break to her as gently as possible the news of her husband's death.

It was her sister Josephine who told her, in broken sentences; veiled hints that revealed in half concealing. Her husband's friend Richards was there, too, near her. It was he who had been in the newspaper office when intelligence of the railroad disaster was received, with Brently Mallard's name leading the list of "killed." He had only taken the time to assure himself of its truth by a second telegram, and had hastened to forestall any less careful, less tender friend in bearing the sad message.

She did not hear the story as many women have heard the same, with a paralyzed inability to accept its significance. She wept at once, with sudden, wild abandonment, in her sister's arms. When the storm of grief had spent itself she went away to her room alone. She would have no one follow her.

There stood, facing the open window, a comfortable, roomy armchair. Into this she sank, pressed down by a physical exhaustion that haunted her body and seemed to reach into her soul.

She could see in the open square before her house the tops of trees that were all aquiver with the new spring life. The delicious breath of rain was in the air. In the street below a peddler was crying his wares. The notes of a distant song which some one was singing reached her faintly, and countless sparrows were twittering in the eaves. There were patches of blue sky showing here and there through the clouds that had met and piled one above the other in the west facing her window.

She sat with her head thrown back upon the cushion of the chair, quite motionless, except when a sob came up into her throat and shook her, as a child who has cried itself to sleep continues to sob in its dreams.

She was young, with a fair, calm face, whose lines bespoke repression and even a certain strength. But now there was a dull stare in her eyes, whose gaze was fixed away off yonder on one of those patches of blue sky. It was not a glance of reflection, but rather indicated a suspension of intelligent thought.

There was something coming to her and she was waiting for it, fearfully. What was it? She did not know; it was too subtle and elusive to name. But she felt it, creeping out of the sky, reaching toward her through the sounds, the scents, the color that filled the air.

Now her bosom rose and fell tumultuously. She was beginning to recognize this thing that was approaching to possess her, and she was striving to beat it back with her will—as powerless as her two white slender hands would have been.

When she abandoned herself a little whispered word escaped her slightly parted lips. She said it over and over under her breath: "free, free, free!" The vacant stare and the look of terror that had followed it went from her eyes. They stayed keen and bright. Her pulses beat fast, and the coursing blood warmed and relaxed every inch of her body.

She did not stop to ask if it were or were not a monstrous joy that held her. A clear and exalted perception enabled her to dismiss the suggestion as trivial. She knew that she would weep again when she saw the kind, tender hands folded in death; the face that had never looked save with love upon her, fixed and gray and dead. But she saw beyond that bitter moment a long procession of years to come that would belong to her absolutely. And she opened and spread her arms out to them in welcome.

There would be no one to live for during those coming years; she would live for herself. There would be no powerful will bending hers in that blind persistence with which men and women believe they have a right to impose a private will upon a fellow-creature. A kind intention or a cruel intention made the act seem no less a crime as she looked upon it in that brief moment of illumination.

And yet she had loved him—sometimes. Often she had not. What did it matter! What could love, the unsolved mystery, count for in the face of this possession of self-assertion which she suddenly recognized as the strongest impulse of her being!

"Free! Body and soul free!" she kept whispering.

Josephine was kneeling before the closed door with her lips to the keyhole, imploring for admission. "Louise, open the door! I beg; open the door—you will make yourself ill. What are you doing, Louise? For heaven's sake open the door."

"Go away. I am not making myself ill." No; she was drinking in a very elixir of life through that open window.

Her fancy was running riot along those days ahead of her. Spring days, and summer days, and all sorts of days that would be her own. She breathed a quick prayer that life might be long. It was only yesterday she had thought with a shudder that life might be long.

She arose at length and opened the door to her sister's importunities. There was a feverish triumph in her eyes, and she carried herself unwittingly like a goddess of Victory. She clasped her sister's waist, and together they descended the stairs. Richards stood waiting for them at the bottom.

Someone was opening the front door with a latchkey. It was Brently Mallard who entered, a little travel-stained, composedly carrying his grip-sack and umbrella. He had been far from the scene of the accident, and did not even know there had been one. He stood amazed at Josephine's piercing cry; at Richards' quick motion to screen him from the view of his wife.

When the doctors came, they said she had died of heart disease—of the joy that kills.

Homework

Task One: Reading

Directions: Read the passage given below and summarize the writing styles (the incident, the details, the point of view, the plot, etc.).

Passage One

My Second Chance for Happiness

Looking back over the past years of my life, I have begun to wonder what I have accomplished of any importance and value, and what I have achieved. In what way has my being here influenced and/or benefited those around me—especially those dear to my heart?

As far back as I can remember, I was always extremely maternal. I was seven years old when my first brother was born, followed years later by the birth of my second brother. Indeed, I was their sister; however, I cared for and loved them as though I were their mother. Of course, being just kids, we all played games and had fun and silly times, but I always felt protective and responsible toward them. Even though we were seven and nine years apart, respectively, I practically brought up my brothers, and for all purposes, they were my sons. I even took care of my sister (two years my senior) and helped her in any way I could.

During my school years and later while in the workplace, I found that any way from home, I worried about my brothers' safety and well-being. To this way, my brothers prove the fact that my love, caring, and guidance had an impact on their lives in very beneficial ways.

I eventually went on to marry, and I became the mother of two daughters. I love being a mom and I know that I devoted 100 percent of myself to raising my children. As normally happens, my daughters grew up, completed their education, and married.

I felt sad and incomplete, and sometimes lost. I realize it was not because they had moved on in their lives, but actually because I had no one to take care of and nurture any longer. I did not feel whole or fulfilled. So I went to work every day, cooked, cleaned, laundered, but something was definitely missing from my life and my heart. My life was to change dramatically when one day my daughter announced her pregnancy. At first, I did not feel anything one way or the other, and I could not begin to imagine how I would feel being a grandmother. On the eventful day when my first grandchild was born, I was given a second chance as happiness wrapped up in pure, innocent, precious gift of love.

Now that I am a grandmother of four, I realize my purpose on earth—to be a loving mother and grandmother in every aspect of these honorable times of life. It all fits together like perfectly matched patches in the quilt of life.

Nothing makes me happier than to see my grandchild growing and progressing and responding to what I teach them with eagerness and love. We have learning times together, and best of all, fun times—when they transport me, heart and soul, to that innocent, youthful world of theirs, filled with wonder, curiosity, and hope.

I may not be a professional success or famous, but we all have our calling in life. I always was a very maternal woman, and at this time in my life, I have found a comforting, rewarding, heartwarming reason to be—I am a grandmother!

In this modern, cold, overly technical, programmed world of ours, nothing can ever rise above or take the place of plain old-fashioned caring, love, and the human touch. No matter how we are forced to achieve higher positions and riches, the most important and precious parts and functions of our lives are free. For me, the innocent tinkle in a small child's eye and the unconditional love that these "tiny people," my grandchildren, so unselfishly lavish upon me is worth more than any treasure on earth.

Passage Two

A Motor Race

The Motor-race was not due to begin until 2:30 and the large crowd cheered loudly when at 2:15 the first cars were wheeled out to take up their positions. So many racing-cars gathered together were a rare and splendid sight. Shining red, blue, and silver in the bright sunshine, they looked rather like jet-aeroplanes without wings. On the course, drivers dressed in helmets were talking to each other or standing by their cars, while engineers checked the engines for the last time. Soon a great many people began arriving at the starting-point and the crowd broke into clapping when the two champions, Mercer and

Torres, arrived on the scene.

At 2:30 sharp there was a pistol-shot followed by a roar of engines. The race had begun and in a few seconds the cars were fighting for the first place. All the cars got off well except No. 5, which refused to start and was hurriedly wheeled off the track.

From the very beginning it seemed as if the race would be entirely between Torres and Mercer, for they were soon in front of the others. A small blue car with an unknown driver at the wheel was following close behind, but was not near enough to offer the champions any serious challenge. The cars flashed by like bullets and there were cheers when Mercer's car took the lead. But this did not last long, for after a while he seemed to be having trouble and he stopped his big silver car to have a wheel changed. Though this was done at great speed, it gave Torres time enough to get well in front. There seemed little chance for Mercer to catch up now. The only car anywhere near Torres was the blue car—until something went wrong with it. On a dangerous bend it got out of control, spun round several times, and shot up the side of the bank. Its driver steered it skillfully back on the course and went on as if nothing had happened. Torres was now over half a lap in front and the race was nearing its end. Mercer was just coming into third place when the blue car moved away at tremendous speed. There were gasps of surprise from the crowd as the unknown driver drew closer and closer to Torres and finally sped past him in the last lap to win the race.

Passage Three

A Frightening Experience

Ann turned into a wing of the house which was quite deserted and silent. At the end of it a shut door confronted her. She opened it softly. It was all dark within. But enough light entered from the corridor to show her the high bookcases ranged against the walls, the position of the furniture, and some dark, heavy curtains at the end. She was the first, then, to come to the meeting. She passed in between them into the recess of a great bow-window, opening on to the park; and a sound, a strange, creaking sound, brought her heart into her mouth.

Someone was already in the room, then. Somebody had been quietly watching as she came in from the lighted corridor. The sound grew louder. Ann peered between the curtains, holding them apart with shaking hands, and through that chink from behind her a vague twilight flowed into the room. In the far corner, near to the door, high up on a tall bookcase, something was clinging—something was climbing down. Whoever it was, having been hiding behind the ornamental top of the heavy mahogany bookcase, was now using the shelves like the rungs of a ladder.

Ann was seized with a panic. A sob broke from her throat. She ran for the door. But she was too late. A black figure dropped from the bookcase to the ground and, as Ann reached out her hands to the door, a scarf was whipped about her mouth, stifling her cry. She was jerked back into the room, but her fingers had touched the light switch by the door, and as she stumbled and fell, the room was lighted up. Her assailant fell upon her, driving the breath out of her lungs, and knotted the scarf tightly at the back of her head. Ann tried to lift herself, and recognized with a gasp of amazement that the assailant who pinned her down by the weight of her body and the thrust of her knees was Francine Rollard. Her panic gave place to anger and a burning humiliation. She fought with all the strength of her supply body. But the scarf about her mouth stifled and weakened her, and with growing dismay she understood that she was no match for the hardy peasant girl. She was the taller of the two, but her height did not avail her; she was like a child matched wild with a cat. Francine's hands were made of steel. She snatched Ann's arms behind her back and bound her wrists, as she lay face downwards, her bosom labouring, her heart racing so that she felt that it must burst. Then, as Ann gave up the contest, she turned and tied her by the ankles.

Task Two: Writing Practice

Directions: Tell a story from the point of view of "I" in around 300 words. Your writing must include the beginning, the development and the conclusion. Pay attention to the characterization, the climax, and the choice of verbs.

Unit Ten

Description

Introductory Remarks

Description is the act, process, or technique of describing by using vivid images to illustrate a specific experience, a person, or a place; it is the method of development in which the writer uses facts and senses to support the point. Description allows a reader to experience something new, to come to a fresh appreciation of the familiar or to perceive the familiar from a fresh perspective.

Description is one of the most frequently used methods of developing our writing because few of us can make it through the day without describing something—a new teacher, an ex-boyfriend, the changeable weather, the latest cell phone, or the new look of a city. Besides pure description, however, we also use description as a part of our essay that is predominantly developed by using some other methods. In narration, for example, we use description to create vividness, to add specific detail, to provide vitality, or to create a context. Regardless of how we use description, it is easy to see that it strengthens an essay considerably.

Warm-Up Exercise

Directions：Read the essay given below and discuss in small groups the points valuable and the points needed to be improved.

Good-Bye

I never imagined leaving home for college would be difficult. I have been away from home many times before. When I was 12, I started going to church camp every summer for a week. When I was 16, I started going as a counselor. By then I was staying for three weeks. When I was a sophomore, I went to Nebraska for three weeks with my best friend and her family. Last year, I went to Mexico for a month on a mission trip and helped build two houses.

I thought going to college would be a snap, but problems started about a week before I left. My mom helped me start packing. The clothes were no problem, but the keepsakes I had to leave behind were. One of my boyfriends won me a bear at the Warren County Fair two years ago. We are still friends, but we don't go out anymore. I would be stupid to take that bear to college. It doesn't mean that much to me. Or at least I didn't think it did, but the thought of leaving it behind hurt. It was like leaving part of me behind.

I also have a small lamp that was my grandmother's. It's very old and delicate. My grandmother had an artificial leg and was nearly blind for several years before she died. By her bedside, she had this lamp that turned on if you touched it. If you touched it again, it went off. It was very handy for my grandmother because she couldn't see well enough to turn a knob or push a button. As a little girl, I used to love to touch the lamp and see it come on. It was like magic to me. When my grandmother died five years ago, she left the lamp to me, knowing how much I had enjoyed it as a little girl. I hadn't given that lamp any thought for a long time, but it was too fragile to take to college and yet leaving it behind was like leaving behind my past.

The most difficult part of saying good-bye, however, was not the packing. The most difficult part was actually leaving. I only live in Warren, so it's not like I was going a long distance. My mom and dad had already made two trips to Titusville and helped me move in gradually. They had attended orientation events with me, and in some ways, it seemed like I had already started school. But there was one thing. I always knew I was going home at the end of the day. And then on the last Sunday in August, after lunch, it was time for me to leave for good. It wasn't that I would never be back, but I would never be back permanently. I would always "live" somewhere else. When I left for Nebraska with my friend, I bolted out of the kitchen without even a look back. But I knew in three weeks I would come home—and that I had a home to come to. Going to college was so difficult because "home" would never be the same. I would be a wanderer in the world until one day I could have my own home. It might take years. And it was scary.

I am an only child, and I know my mom and dad were as emotional as I was the day I left. I was determined not to cry. I know it would have made them feel worse. After lunch, I grabbed a few last minute items and bounced out the door telling them I would be in touch. I didn't even kiss them because I knew I'd break down if I did. I pulled out of the driveway, gave them a big smile and a wave and drove off. But I broke down in tears before I had gone 200 yards. I had a long, long cry on the way to Titusville that day.

Of course things are better now. I still have a wave of homesickness coming over me at times. And I still have plenty of days when I wish I could be the little girl I once was. But since I can't, I'm trying to become someone better.

Section One: Introduction to Descriptive Essay

Purposes

The purpose of a descriptive essay is to describe a person, a place, or a thing so that your reader can see, hear, feel, taste, or smell what you are describing. Some of the concrete purposes you might have for the descriptive essay might include: to please, to inform, and to support other methods of development or reinforce the main point.

To please: A good essay arouses the reader's senses and has an impact on his mind—evoking the correct response. The writer succeeds if he is able to capture the reader's attention and retain it till the end. A good descriptive essay should lure the reader and entice him to read without stopping.

To inform means the writer uses description to inform the reader of the perception or to enable the reader to understand the effects the perception has on him or her. And both achieve the purpose of putting the reader to have access to a new awareness.

To support other methods of development or reinforce the main point: for this purpose, description is not used as the primary method of development but something that helps other rhetorical modes: for example, in a narrative essay, description can make the setting or characters more vivid. In an analysis, description can help us highlight the essential differences between two items we are discussing.

Principles

A descriptive essay has one clear dominant impression. If, for example, you are describing the changes of China since the introduction of the reform and opening up policy, it is important for you to decide and let your reader know whether it has been changing for the good or for the bad; in order to have one dominant impression it cannot be both. The dominant impression guides the author's selection of detail and is thereby made clear to the reader in the thesis statement.

A descriptive essay can be objective or subjective, giving the author a wide choice of tone, diction and attitude. Objective information are factual statements about the real qualities of the subject mainly answering the questions of who, what, when, where, and why. For instance, an objective description of one's dog would mention such facts as height, weight, color and so forth. While subjective information are statements about the writer's impression of the subject in language rich in modifiers, figures of speech, and in describing the senses of touch, taste, sight, hearing, and smell. For example, a subjective description about a dog would stress the author's feelings toward the dog, as well as its personality and habits.

The purpose of a purely descriptive essay is to involve the reader so that he or she can actually visualize the things being described. Therefore, it is important to use specific and concrete details. While giving details, focus on different aspects in different paragraphs depending on its content. In this way the essay reads well, coherent and meaningful. Care must be taken to be as logical as possible with important details preceding minor ones, or broader details preceding specific ones.

Conventions

The descriptive essay relies on concrete, specific details to communicate its point. Description can incorporate all the senses, or can focus on just one. If you do focus on just one sensual impression, you should give a reason to the reader for your narrow focus.

The author of a descriptive essay must carefully select details to support the dominant impression. In other words, the author has the license to omit details which are incongruent with the dominant impression unless the dominant impression is one which points out the discrepancies.

Description very often relies on emotion and on our experiences to convey its point. Because of this, verbs, adverbs, and adjectives convey more to the reader than nouns do. An incorporation of verbs, adjectives, and adverbs helps build an emotional state, and reflection of our experience and knowledge of the world.

Strategies for Developing the Descriptive Essay

Be subtle. Try giving all the details first; the dominant impression then is built from these details.

Be consistent. Make sure your details are consistent with the dominant impression. Reread your description to ensure that each one of your smaller details is indeed supporting the dominant impression.

Be systematic. Move your reader through space and time chronologically (such as from front to back, beginning to end, left to right, top to bottom, interior to exterior, smallest to largest, start to destination). For instance, you might want to describe a train ride from start to destination, or a stream from its source to where it joins the river.

Be aware of change. Use a then-and-now approach to show decay, change, or improvement. The house where you grew up might now be a rambling shack. The variations on this strategy are endless.

Be emotional. Select an emotion and try to describe it. Choose an emotion to be a dominant theme in your description. Organize and select details around that dominant emotion. It might be more difficult to get started, but it can be worthwhile.

Section Two: Structure of Descriptive Essay

The Introduction

The main task of the introduction of a descriptive essay is to develop a topic sentence which states the controlling idea (central impression)—the most important thing to convey to your reader, and to list the major factors that lead to it, and which you are supposed to cover in the body as evidence to support the controlling idea.

Although the topic sentence can be located at the beginning, in the middle or at the end of the introduction paragraph, it is advisable for you to put the topic sentence at the very beginning for that helps get your subject into focus and your description under control.

And the method in developing a qualified topic sentence might be as follows: Write one clearly worded topic sentence which identifies your subject and states your attitude, thus stating your central impression. Put the topic sentence first in the paragraph. Make sure that every detail in the body of the paragraph contributes to the topic sentence.

Mini-task: *Topic Sentence Development*

Directions: The following description of George Washington as a young man creates a definite impression. Read these details carefully and develop a topic sentence to convey the central impression.

Details about George Washington:

Straight as an Indian, measuring 6 feet 2 inches in his stockings, and weighing 175 pounds

Well-developed muscles, indicating great strength

A well-shaped head, gracefully poised on a superb neck

Blue-gray, penetrating eyes overhung by a heavy brow

A face that terminated in a good, firm chin

A pleasing and benevolent though a commanding countenance, regular and placid features with all the muscles of his face under perfect control, though flexible and expressive of deep feeling when moved by emotion

Deliberate and engaging in conversation, looks you full in the face

Graceful movements, a majestic walk

The Body

In dealing with the body, what you are expected to do is to provide details to support or prove the topic sentence. Remember certain details will create certain impressions. In order to convey the central impression expressed in the topic sentence, all the details you may cover in the body must be closely related to the central impression. To achieve this purpose, you've got to ask yourself "what does all of this information add up to the central impression? Any details that do not contribute to conveying the central impression should be excluded. "

Selecting Details

Once you have developed a central impression in the introduction, select the descriptive details that will best convey this impression to your reader. The details selected should not only be able to support your central impression as expressed in the topic sentence, they should also be concrete and visual.

Detail-selection is necessary because whatever or whoever we describe, there are so many details for us to choose from, and the fact is that we are unable to cover all the details available. Take the description of your grandmother as an example, if you tried to include every detail about her, the result would be an unwieldy descriptive essay. But how do we decide what to include and what to omit? One part of the answer is selecting details to support the central impression as developed in the topic sentence; another part of the answer is depending on the audience and purpose; still another is to settle on one impression of your subject and describe features that contribute to that impression. For example, if your grandmother is interesting because she is enthusiastic, eccentric, and young-at-heart, decide which of these three qualities will be your focus and then describe the only features that convey that impression.

Mini-task: *Reading and Writing*

Directions: Read the following paragraph, and then write out what your most impression is on this description.

The Fruit Cellar

It was late last night as I reluctantly took the steps down to the gloomy fruit cellar. Its dark, dusty shelves were located behind the crumbling basement walls. I fumbled in the dark for the lifeless screw-in light bulb and managed to twist it to a faint glow. With that the musty room was dimly lit, and long dark shadows lurked on the ceiling, picturing enlarged, misshapen jars of fruit. Water condensed and dripped from the ceiling, shattering the eerie silence. Cobwebs suspended in every corner hid their makers in a gray crisscross of lines. Hesitantly I took a step, my sneakers soaking up the black water lying 2 inches deep on the floor. A rat darted through a hole in the wall, and jars of fruit peered at me with their glassy eyes. The rotting shelves looked as if at any moment they would fall to the floor. The cold, gray walls reminded me of an Egyptian tomb forgotten long ago. Yet mummies didn't decay, and I distinctly smelled the odor of something rotting.

Using Concrete Sensory Details

Concrete sensory details refer to specific words that appeal to the senses (sight, sound, taste, smell, and touch). If you look back at "The Fruit Cellar" you will notice many vivid image with concrete sensory details. Take, for example, the sentence, "Cobwebs suspended in every corner hid their makers in a gray crisscross of lines." The detail here is sensory because it appeals to the sense of sight. It is also concrete because of such specific words as suspended and crisscross of lines. Hence a clear picture is created in the mind of the reader, a picture much more vivid than one that would be formed from description like "cobwebs were in every corner hiding their spiders."

Notice too in "The Fruit Cellar" where the writer employs more than just the sense of sight. He also includes sound (water "shattering the eerie silence"), smell ("the odor of something rotting"), and touch ("feeling the dampness at my back"). While it is true that description typically relies more on one sense, impressions are most clearly conveyed when the writer brings in as many senses as possible that are pertinent to what is being described. As you can see from the above analysis, concrete sensory details help to make scenes realistic and memorable, help readers experience an emotion, share feelings more clearly, and make them feel like they are on the scene.

Mini-task: *Reading and Response*

Directions: The following passage describes a pivotal scene from George Orwell's famous essay "Shooting an Elephant," which focuses on the use and abuse of power. Notice how Orwell draws on the sense of touch, hearing, and sight.

Shooting an Elephant

When I pulled the trigger I did not hear the bang or feel the kick—one never does when a shot goes home—but I heard the devilish roar of glee that went up from the crowd. In that instant, in too short a time, one would have thought, even for the bullet to get there, a mysterious, terrible change had come over the elephant. He neither stirred nor fell, but every line of his body had altered. He looked suddenly stricken, shrunken, immensely old, as though the frightful impact of the bullet had paralyzed him without knocking him down. At last, after what seemed a long time—it might have been five seconds, I dare say—he sagged flabbily to his knees. His mouth slobbered.

Arranging Details

Once you have chosen the best details to fit your purpose, you must arrange them in a logical order. No matter what your paragraph describes—an object, a person, a location, or an event—you cannot list details at random. There must be a pattern. When you observe something, you get a picture of the whole thing, but the order in which you think about its different parts or effects does not really matter, because the reader cannot visualize the whole as you did. You must therefore provide a pattern into which the reader can fit the details and recreate the whole in his or her own imagination.

The main pattern of organization in descriptive writing is space order, or spatial arrangement. You arrange details in an order that the eye might easily follow: top to bottom, left to right, far to near, and so on. Your location in relation to what you are describing can help you arrange details effectively. From a fixed position, your eyes can sweep around a room, scan an object from top to bottom, examine a person from head to toe, or contemplate a landscape from the horizon to where you are standing. You may even choose a particular or unique characteristic and extend your pattern of details outward from it. If you are in motion, you can form your impressions as objects come into view, as you pass something, or even as you walk around it. Details must be arranged to give your reader the view that you had as an actual observer.

Mini-task: *Reading and Discussion*

Directions: Read the passage given below and discuss in small groups how one student describes a special kind of room.

The Locker Room

John Navage

One of the most distinctive, and perhaps most easily recognizable, atmospheres is that of an athlete's locker room. As you enter, the unmistakable odor of perspiring bodies, damp leather, and dirty clothes hits you; it is a familiar one for the athlete, but sometimes unbearable for others. The room is usually large, dim, and long enough to be lined with rows of army-green lockers. The dryers hum in the background while the steam from the showers settles and penetrates every nook and cranny, making the floor and walls seem dripping wet. We bring our emotions into this sanctuary, away from prying eyes and ears, to release our joys and jubilation, disappointments and discouragements, and sometimes our tears. The language would make an English professor cringe, yet nothing could ever change it. It may sound offensive in many respects, but to an athlete it is part of his life that he cherishes and never forgets when those days are set aside for a different kind of life.

Conclusion

The conclusion of a descriptive paragraph should therefore be a detail of observation which permanently fixes that central impression in the imagination of the reader. The conclusion is not just a way to bring your paragraph to a close; it is a final opportunity to create the desired effect on your reader. Here the details may be drawn together to provide a final unifying impression. Your conclusion should restate or reinforce your general impression, the attitude in your topic sentence.

Mini-task: *Writing*

Directions: Write a descriptive paragraph of around 150 words on whatever topic you are interested in. You are expected to write one clearly worded topic sentence which identifies your subject and states your attitude, and to support the central impression in the body with carefully selected details. Make sure that every detail in the body contributes to the topic sentence.

Homework

Task One: Writing

Directions: Write a descriptive essay of around 300 words on whatever topic you like. You are expected to write one clearly worded topic sentence which identifies your subject and states your attitude, thus stating your central impression. Support or prove the central impression with carefully selected concrete details arranged in logical order. Make sure that every detail in the body contributes to the topic sentence. Draw a natural and reasonable conclusion based on previous description.

Task Two: Reading and Response

Directions: Read the passages given below and prepare a three-minute presentation about the descriptive skills used respectively in each passage.

Passage One

One Scene in Hyde Park

Loud shouting in the distance made us look up. This was nothing unusual for Hyde Park, for many people come here on a Sunday to air their views, and shouting is the only means by which they can make themselves heard. We had become part of a large crowd which moved from speaker to speaker to hear what each one had to say. So far, we had listened to political speeches, serious debates, and lonely singers wailing dolefully to themselves. Now the newcomer attracted our attention, mainly because of the extreme loudness of his voice.

We soon discovered that the cause of all this commotion was certainly the ugliest fellow we had ever seen. He was completely bald and his face was painted red and blue so that he looked rather like a Red Indian chieftain. When a reasonable crowd had gathered, the man quietened down, surveyed everybody with some contempt, and proceeded to undo his shirt. Soon he was displaying a huge, coloured tattoo which covered the whole of his back and chest. When the man was satisfied that he had produced the desired effect on the crowd, he explained quite plainly that he was a burglar and wanted to say a few words about his trade. He commenced by criticizing the police severely for impeding him in his work. Policemen, he explained, were ungrateful to him, because it was people like himself who kept them busy. These remarks so astonished the crowd, that it drew round him closer, anxious to hear more. The man began describing the art of getting through a closed window at night, when a formidable old lady shook her umbrella at him and said that if he did not go away, she would call a policeman. The burglar calmly pointed out that the police were his friends, and only took an interest in him when he was about his "lawful" work. Glaring at the crowd, he said that if anyone else had any further comments to make, he would be glad to meet him in the dark. The crowd laughed uneasily, but the old lady stalked off angrily to fetch a policeman. We waited expectantly to see what would happen as the burglar continued to explain how easy it was to pick a lock with a hairpin.

Passage Two

Monk's House

There was one thing that I found rather strange on my first day at Monk's House. The floors in the house were very thin. The bathroom was directly above the kitchen, and when

Mrs. Woolf was having her bath before breakfast, I could hear her talking to herself. On and on she went, talked, talked, talked, asking questions and giving herself answers. I thought there must be two or three people up there with her. When Mr. Woolf saw that I looked surprised, he told me that Mrs. Woolf always said the sentences out loud that she had written during the night. She needed to know if they sounded right and the bath was a good place for trying them out.

I was not allowed to make coffee at Monk's House—Mr. and Mrs. Woolf were very particular about coffee and always made it themselves—so Mr. Woolf came into the kitchen at eight o'clock every morning to make it. When we carried breakfast to Mrs. Woolf's room I noticed that she had always been working during the night. There were pencils and paper beside her bed so that she woke up and she could work, and sometimes it seemed as though she had had very little sleep.

Mrs. Woolf's bedroom was outside the house in the garden; I used to think how inconvenient it must be to have to go out in the rain or to go to bed. Her bedroom had been added onto the back of the house; the door faced the garden and a window at the side opened out on to a field. I remember that a cow came one night and put its head in through the window. It amused Mrs. Woolf very much, but in case it happened again Mr. Woolf bought the field and added part of it to the garden. Because the writing-room was small, he had a larger one built for her at the end of the garden against the church wall.

I can always remember her coming to the house each day from her writing-room, when I rang the bell for lunch at one o'clock she used to walk down through the garden smoking one of her favourite cigarettes in a long holder. She was tall and thin and very graceful. She had large, deep-set eyes and a wide curving mouth—I think perhaps it was this that made her face seem particularly beautiful. She wore long skirts—usually blue or brown—in the fashion of the day, and silk jackets of the same colour. I remember too, there was always a large silk handkerchief folded into the jacket pocket.

Her cigarettes were made from a special tobacco called *My Mixture*. Mr. Woolf bought it for her in London, and, in the evening, they used to sit by the fire and make these cigarettes themselves. It was a mild, sweet-smelling tobacco, and she would not have any other cigarettes.

Mrs. Woolf wore clothes that suited her well. I pressed them for her and did any sewing that was necessary—she was not able to sew, although sometimes she liked to try. There was one thing in the kitchen that Mrs. Woolf was very good at doing; she could make beautiful bread. I was surprised how complicated it was and how exactly Mrs. Woolf carried it out. She returned three or four times in a morning to work at it. Finally she made it into the shape of a cottage loaf and baked it at just the right temperature.

Passage Three

Edinburgh

Edinburgh, the capital of Scotland, is a fine old city built partly in the valley of the River Leith and partly on the rolling hills which surround it. The city is dominated by the castle, an ancient fortress standing on the summit of a massive rock, which has been the scene of many battles and sieges throughout centuries of Scottish history. Today what remains of the original castle is preserved as a museum piece and a home for military relics.

The road from the castle to the royal palace of Holyroodhouse is known as The Royal Mile. It is a very old thoroughfare running through the oldest part of the city where there are many famous historic houses and narrow lanes called Closes. The newer part of the city lies north of the famous Princes Street, which is the widest and most impressive of the many wide streets, elegant squares and imposing terraces that are to be found in Edinburgh.

The trains bringing visitors to Edinburgh run right into the heart of the city. Climbing up the steps from Waverley Station, the visitor is greeted by a blaze of colour in Princes Street Gardens and a splendid view down the mile-long length of Princes Street itself. The grey stone buildings that line one side of Princes Street have been described as a series of palaces; they are, in fact, department stores and shops. In some shops you can see beautiful displays of Scottish tartans and woollens, and tempting arrangements of shortbread, Edinburgh rock and, of course, Scotch whisky. About half way along Princes Street is the tallest spire in the city—a monumental memorial to Sir Walter Scott—and a little farther on is the Floral Clock. This unique clock, made entirely of growing flowers, is always in full bloom during the Edinburgh Festival.

For three weeks every summer, Edinburgh is alive with exhilarated festival-goers and performers who come from all over the world, and the city is gay with flags and decorations. This international festival of the arts fills every theatre, concert hall, exhibition gallery and assembly room with performances of opera, dancing, music, plays, revues, films, puppet shows and recitals, and specially-mounted exhibitions of painting and sculpture. The festival is not limited to indoor activities: every weekday the noise of the city's traffic is lost in the sound of music as the Scottish pipers march along Princes Street with kilts swinging and drums beating. But the most spectacular event of the festival is undoubtedly the military tattoo. This takes place under searchlights on the Castle esplanade—the scene of many executions in the past—with the floodlit castle in the background. Nowhere could one find a natural setting more impressive and appropriate.

Unit Eleven

Argumentation

Introductory Remarks

An argument is a written or spoken text that expresses a point of view with the purpose of influencing the opinions of readers. Sometimes arguments can be aggressive, composed deliberately to change what readers believe, think, or do. At other times your goals may be more subtle, and your writing may be designed to convince others that specific facts are reliable or that certain views should be considered or at least tolerated. Although many arguments are aimed at winning, there are types of argument, such as arguments to inform, to convince, to explore, and to make decisions.

In writing argumentation, you need to know how to put yourself in the position of the reader so that you can get your own points across while anticipating and addressing the reactions of potential readers. You need to know how to question and disagree to the points being made in the argument. Otherwise, you may end up writing reports, rather than arguments. You need to know how to make claims, attach reasons, offer evidence, and use qualifiers, or your argument can not be convincing and responsible. Because of all these requirements, writing an effective argument poses big and demanding challenges for most of us.

Warm-Up Exercise

Directions: Read the following passage and discuss in small groups the purpose of the argument and the skills of argumentation.

Two Glasses of Wine

When things in your life seem almost too much to handle, when 24 hours in a day is not enough, remember the mayonnaise jar and the 2 glasses of wine...

A professor stood before his philosophy class and had some items in front of him. When the class began, wordlessly, he picked up a very large and empty mayonnaise jar and proceeded to fill it with golf balls.

He then asked the students if the jar was full. They agreed that it was. The professor then picked up a box of pebbles and poured them into the jar. He shook the jar lightly. The pebbles rolled into the open areas between the golf balls. He then asked the students again if the jar was full. They agreed it was. The professor next picked up a box of sand and poured it into the jar. Of course, the sand filled up everything else. He asked once more if the jar was full. The students responded with a unanimous "yes." The professor then produced two glasses of wine from under the table and poured the entire contents into the jar, effectively filling the empty space between the sand. The students laughed. "Now," said the professor, as the laughter subsided, "I want you to recognize that this jar represents your life. The golf balls are the important things: your family, your children, your health, your friends, and your favorite passions; things that if everything else was lost and only they remained, your life would still be full. The pebbles are the other things that matter like your job, your house, and your car. The sand is everything else; the small stuff. If you put the sand into the jar first," he continued, "there is no room for the pebbles or the golf balls. The same goes for life. If you spend all your time and energy on the small stuff, you will never have room for the things that are important to you.

Pay attention to the things that are critical to your happiness. Play with your children. Take time to get medical checkups. Take your partner out to dinner. Play another 18. There will always be time to clean the house and fix the disposal. Take care of the golf balls first; the things that really matter. Set your priorities. The rest is just sand. "

One of the students raised her hand and inquired what the wine represented. The professor smiled. "I am glad you asked. It just goes to show you that no matter how full your life may seem, there's always room for a couple of glasses of wine with a friend. "

Introduction to the Structure of Arguments

Section One: Making Claims

Begin your arguments with claims, which are statements of belief or truth. When you make an argument, you stake out a position others will likely find controversial and debatable. For example, the gap between the rich and the poor has been becoming smaller since the reform and open policy in China; The price of commodity house will go down in China; The English enhancement program is a great success.

Notice that when you make a claim, the arguments depend on conditions set by others— your audience or readers. The claim you make should be worth arguing, which means the claim tends to be controversial. There is no point insisting on what most people acknowledge. For example, China is a country with the largest population in the world. Also claims should be debatable, which means that they can be demonstrated using logic or evidence, or materials offered to support an argument. For example, the claim "I feel uncomfortable today" is not a debatable claim because no one can challenge your feeling.

Mini-task: *Making Claims*

Directions: Read the samples and work out a list of claims that tend to be controversial and debatable. Discuss the claim list in small groups. Sample claims:

1. Parents should accept responsibility and be punished if their children behave badly.
2. It is unfair to cover celebrities' private lives in the mass media.
3. Students cannot acquire qualifications and qualities essential to success through university education.

Section Two: Attaching Reasons

Once a claim is made, you are expected to support or develop the claim by providing reasons. Most often one reason is not enough to convince the reader or the audience, and you are expected to draw up a list of reasons to fully develop your claim. One student writer, for instance, wanted to gather a list of reasons in support of a claim that his college campus needed more space for car parking. He had been doing some research—gathering statistics about parking space allocation, numbers of car drivers using particular parking lots, and numbers of cars registered on campus. Before he went further with this argument, however, he decided to make a list of the reasons he had identified for more car parking space:

Personal experience: At least twice a week for two terms, he had been unable to find a parking space for his car.

Anecdotes: Several of his classmates told similar stories; one had even sold her car as a result.

Facts: He had found out that the number of cars and the parking lot allocated to parking is not in reasonable proportion. Only 56 percent of the cars registered are allowed in the parking lot on campus.

Authorities: The campus police chief in charge of car parking had indicated in an interview with the college newspaper that she believed a problem existed for students trying to park cars.

Mini-task: *Attaching Reasons*

Directions: Individually work out a list of possible reasons in support of one of the given claims below and then discuss the reasons in small groups:

1. Reasons for being single.
2. Health is more important than wealth.
3. Chinese replaces English as a universal language.
4. Why am I living off campus?
5. People are never satisfied with what they have.

Section Three: Determining Warrants

The warrant is the connection, often unstated and assumed, between your claim and your supporting reason(s), the glue that holds them together. Like the warrant in legal situations, a sound warrant in an argument gives you authority to proceed with a case. If readers accept your warrant, you can then present specific evidence to prove your claim. If readers dispute your warrant, you'll have to defend it before you can move on to the claim itself.

The warrant is the assumption that makes the claim seem plausible. Let's demonstrate this logical movement with an easy example.

Smoking in public should be prohibited (claim).

Smoking in public does great harm to second-hand smokers (reason).

If something is harmful to others, it should not be allowed (warrant).

Mini-task: *Determining Warrants*

Directions: State the warrants that support particular arguments by following the previous examples. You can either take the arguments given below as claims or work out your own claims.

1. We should not encourage teenagers to travel alone.
2. One couple, one child policy should not be abolished.
3. Advertisements exerting negative effects on the youth should be banned.
4. Students should not be allowed to bring their cell phone into the classroom.
5. Death penalty should be more strictly controlled in China.

Section Four: Offering Evidence

Claims and warrants are only the skeleton of an argument; the bulk of a writer's work—the richest, most interesting part—still remains to be done after the argument has been assembled. Evidence you offer in support of a warrant is called backing. For example:

Warrant

What unifies the nation ought to be a national priority.

Backing

China wants to be a member of world powers to have its voice heard on world affairs. (Emotional claim)

A country as regionally, nationally, and culturally diverse as China needs common purposes and values to hold its people together. (Ethical claim)

In the last two decades, the advancement in engineering technology and space information, the development in nuclear science and technology, and the rapid growth in economy has enabled Chinese people to work toward common goals. (Logical claim)

Mini-task: *Offering Evidence*

Directions: Offer evidence to support the following claims:

1. Preferring men to women has its roots in Chinese culture.
2. Tourism is relatively a quicker way for developing countries to garner foreign exchange.
3. Living in the country is a better choice than living in the city.
4. The respect for the elderly is often a comfortable slogan today.
5. The government should encourage a certain percentage of high level jobs to be reserved for women.

Section Five: Using Qualifiers

Qualifiers are terms and conditions that limit your claims and warrants. The application of qualifiers during the process of writing can save time and make the argument easier and more convincing. One way to qualify an argument is by spelling out the terms of the claim as precisely as possible. Never assume that readers understand the limits you have in mind. Whenever you can, spell out what you mean precisely. You'll have less work to do as a result. In the following examples, the first claim in each pair would be much harder to argue convincingly and responsibly—and tougher to research—than the second claim.

Example 1:

Efforts to prohibit smoking in public have failed. (Unqualified claim)

Most efforts in Beijing to prohibit smoking in restaurants have failed. (Qualified claim)

Example 2:

Welfare programs should be cut. (Unqualified claim)

Ineffective government welfare programs should be identified, modified, and, if necessary, eliminated. (Qualified claim)

Experienced writers cherish qualifying expressions because they make writing more precise and honest.

Qualifiers

few / a few	it is possible
rarely / seldom	it seems
some / some more	it may be
sometimes / on occasion	more or less
in some cases	many / a lot of
in the main / mainly	routinely / regularly
most / the majority	one might argue
often / frequently	perhaps / possibly
under these conditions	as the case may be
for the most part	if it were so
for the better part	generally / wholly

Homework

Task One: Writing

Directions: Write an argumentative composition on "Who Should Take Care of Our Seniors" in around 200 words.

Task Two: Reading and Response

Directions: Decide whether the following passages are argumentations. If the passage does not explain why, and go to the next. If it does, then indicate the conclusion, premise(s), and issue. You may simply cite the number to indicate conclusion and premise(s).

1. (1) Carlos must be sick today. (2) He did not show up for work. (3) And he has never missed work unless he is sick.

2. （1）Students should attend class regularly and punctually. （2）Our research shows that there is a direct correlation between good grades and regular class attendance.

3. （1）The last person we hired from Bayview Tech turned out to be a bad employee. （2）I'm not willing to hire anybody else from that school again.

4. （1）And here comes the question of whether it is better to be loved rather than feared, or feared rather than loved; （2）It might be answered that we should wish to be both; but （3）since love and fear can hardly exist together, if we must choose between them, （4）it is far safer to be feared than loved. （5）For of men it may generally be affirmed that they are thankless, fickle, false, studious to avoid danger, greedy of gain, devoted to you while you confer benefits upon them, and （6）ready, while the need is remote, to shed their blood, and sacrifice their property, their lives, and their children for you. （7）But, when danger comes near they turn against you.

5. （1）Marriage has always been a very different thing for men and for women. （2）The two sexes are necessary to each other, but this necessity has never brought about a condition of reciprocity between them. （3）Women have never constituted a caste making exchanges and contracts with the male caste upon a footing of equality. （4）A man is socially an independent and complete individual. （5）He is regarded first of all as a producer whose existence is justified by the work he does for the group. （6）The reproductive and domestic role to which woman is confined has not guaranteed her an equal dignity.

6. （1）Paul Kennedy's *The Rise and Fall of the Great Powers* has had a remarkable impact in the United States since its publication late last year. （2）It has been widely and almost universally favorably reviewed. （3）Its arguments have been discussed in editorials and opinion columns. （4）One major national magazine ran excerpts as its cover story, while another called it the "book of the year."

7. （1）Television has a disastrous impact on children. （2）It appears to be shortening the attention span of the young. （3）It also seems to be eroding their linguistic powers and ability to handle mathematical symbolism. （4）Television also causes them to be increasingly impatient with deferred gratification. （5）Even more serious, television is opening all of society's secrets and taboos, thus erasing the dividing line between childhood and adulthood...

8. （1）In one half of all traffic deaths in the United States, the driver has been drinking. （2）One third of the pedestrians struck and killed by cars were drunk. Driving while intoxicated, or DWI, is illegal in every state. （3）In most states, it is illegal to drive a

car if the Blood Alcohol Content is 0. 1 percent or greater. (4) In most states, it is illegal to drink alcohol while driving. (5) In some states, it is against the law to have an open container of any alcoholic drink in the car.

Task Three: *Reading and Response*

Directions: Read the passages given below and summarize the writing skills. You are also expected to make comments on the points valuable and the points you think could be improved to make a more logical and convincing argumentation.

Passage One

Reasons for Being Single

One of the best reasons for being single is the freedom it gives you to spend your own money in your own way. Wine, women and song—in that order seem to figure large in male expenditure, while clothes, cosmetics and males seem to account for a great deal of female salaries.

The other good reason for being single is the amount of free time you have to enjoy in any way you prefer. Not for singles the chores of family shopping and doing odd jobs about the house. Not for them the worries about baby-sisters to get one night out a week.

Singles are free to spend their time just as the mood takes them. They can roller skate; go to pictures; explore old ruins or just sit with their feet up and enjoy the innocent sin of being completely indolent. They can get up when they like and go to bed when they like. Eat where, what and when they fancy. And meet whoever they like as often as they like.

Passage Two

Childless and Free

In the past, young married couples often had children right after getting married. They didn't ask themselves if they had the desire to stay up at night with babies, to spend a good part of their time with children, to give up going out at night whenever they wanted to. Now, many young couples feel that not having children will allow them to have a freer, more enjoyable life style.

Never has the question of family size attracted as much attention in this country as it is getting now. In this time of "the pill" women's liberation, and high prices, young couples are giving serious thought to the number of children they want, can afford or can raise successfully.

What are the emotional or financial problems of raising a big family? Does raising children become incompatible with a wife's working career in the outside world? Can a childless couple achieve lasting satisfaction on their own?

Michael Shandrik, 29, and his wife Pamela, 31, for example, have joined the growing number of young couples who don't have, and don't want children. Many of their close friends are childless and plan to remain that way. Michael says the decision not to have children developed over four years of marriage. He explains, "We never decided to become childless. It more or less became an understanding after we got married." Pamela adds, "If I had married before 23, I probably would have had children. But as the years went by, I got used to the idea of working and not having children. It is too late to change now."

For both of them, the desire for a free life-style played a big part in the decision. Michael, who wants to build a career in communication, makes the point honestly, "We are just too selfish to have children at this point. We would rather buy the things we want than go without things for the sake of the children. If we had a kid, we would have to start thinking about its education and health. We like the independence of getting up and going somewhere we want. I want to get ahead."

Pamela, too, is concerned about her career. But she also speaks about the need to prevent overpopulation. She says she is a supporter of Zero Population Growth, and adds, "I am doing my part to keep the world from being overcrowded with human beings in another 100 years. Furthermore, from women's point of view, if you have children when you are young, there is a 50 to 50 chance you will be raising them alone. I know a lot of divorced women with children. It is hard for them to raise their children alone."

Thus the decision has been made to remain childless.

Unit Twelve

Exposition

第十二单元　说　明　法

要点提示：说明文的应用可谓广泛，如说明事理、阐述流程、解释制作方法、告知获取信息的步骤，等等。说明文的结构包括：主题句段落——引出说明对象；主体段落——阐述说明对象；收尾段落——总结说明对象。说明的方法多种多样：描述法、顺序法、比较对照法、原因结果法以及问题解析法等，各种方法可单独或混同使用。好的说明文有赖于作者对说明对象的深入了解，对文章结构的合理安排，对说明方法的有效运用和对语言的驾驭能力。

Introductory Remarks

Exposition is a type of oral or written discourse that explains, clarifies, informs, defines, or instructs. When doing expository writing, the writer cannot assume that the reader or listener has prior knowledge or understanding of the topic that is being discussed. Instead, he is expected to teach, inform, reveal and/or amplify ideas and knowledge. To achieve this purpose, he must group ideas, select the best examples, and/or structure his explanation in a manner that is clear and convincing to his audience. And he must explain the relationships and connections between ideas through examples, facts, or anecdotes. The key to writing an effective expository text is for the writer to have a clear understanding of the purpose (mode), the best form (product) to use to get this idea across, and the way to best present the ideas (organizational structures).

You will realize the importance of expositive writing when you think about the type of writing that most of us encounter in our daily life. When you pick up and read a non-fiction book, magazines, or newspaper articles, the author uses expository writing to inform you, the reader, of the topic. At school, students are required to submit school exams and research papers as a means for their teachers to grade their progress. Finally, at work, people are required to produce business reports and memorandums to inform their superiors and co-workers of the occurrences that take place at other levels of the company. In addition, oral exposition is primarily observed in oral academic presentations, business talks, and speeches that are delivered to a group of people. As each of these different cases illustrates, expository writing surrounds us in our everyday lives and frequently serves us the purposes given below: analyze another piece of writing; define a term; describe the procedure; describe how to; discuss an answer; explain how to; explain a facet of reality; explain the procedure used; explain a process or opinion; give directions; give information; provide detailed explanations; present facts and data; tell what happened, etc.

Warm-Up Exercise: Reading and Discussion

Directions: Read the following passage of exposition and discuss in small groups the purpose(s) and writing styles.

How to Make a Simple Birthday Cake

By Sarah Eibon

Have you ever wanted to make a birthday cake for a loved one? Well, here is how to make a simple birthday cake. All you'll need is a little time, love, and a few items from the grocery store.

You will need a boxed cake mix (the favorite of the birthday person), shortening, eggs, oil, flour, and birthday candles (the number will depend on the age of the birthday person). When you get home, you will need to gather a few items: a large mixing bowl, a large cake pan, an electric mixer or a large mixing spoon, a spatula, and measuring cups and spoons.

First, you will need to wash your hands and work area. Read through the directions on the cake box to be sure you have everything you need. Then, gather all of your equipment and food items in your work area, organize it according to the order you will use them in making your cake. Be sure to preheat your oven to the appropriate temperature before you begin.

Next, put the dry cake mix into your large mixing bowl. Then, put the prescribed amount of water, oil, and eggs into the mix. Then, with the electric mixer or mixing spoon mix the batter until it is smooth and free of clumps. Next, grease the large cake pan with the shortening. If you wish, you can wrap your fingers with wax paper to keep them from getting greasy. Then, flour the pan lightly. If you do this over the garbage can it will be easier to clean your work area later. Next, pour the cake batter into the cake pan, using the rubber spatula to scrape all of the batter off the sides of the bowl. Be sure the batter is level in the pan so it will rise evenly. Next, place the cake on the top rack of the oven and bake for the amount of time specified on the box, the time is usually around thirty minutes. While the cake is baking, clean up your work area.

After the cake is done, remove it from the oven. If you push a toothpick to the bottom and it comes out clean, it is done. Turn off the oven and let the cake cool. After the cake has had ample time to cool, you are ready to spread the icing on the cake. If you use a spatula rather than a knife, the icing will spread easier and will be less likely to ruin the cake. When the icing is on the cake, place the appropriate number of birthday candles on it, and you are ready to present your simple birthday cake.

There you have it, a birthday cake that someone will be glad to devour. This cake is easy to make, but still shows someone you care. Be sure to prepare it with love, and your loved one will appreciate it.

Section One: Organization Patterns for Expository Writing

In order to give you more information about written exposition we have provided you with five different examples of expository organizational patterns. You will find that most of them are very familiar to you. But you may have never really considered them to be "kind" of organizational patterns. As you read through them try to figure out how many you find yourself already using in writing on a daily basis.

Pattern One：*Description*

The author describes a topic by listing characteristics, features, and examples.

Sample Passage

The Olympic symbol consists of five interlocking rings. They represent the five continents—Africa, Asia, Europe, America and Oceania—from which athletes come to compete in the games. The rings are colored black, blue, green, red, and yellow. At least one of these colors is found in the flag of every country sending athletes to compete in the Olympic Games.

Pattern Two：*Sequence*

The author lists items or events in numerical or chronological order.

Sample Passage

The Olympic Games began as athletic festivals to honor the Greek gods. The most important festival was held in the valley of Olympia to honor Zeus, the king of the gods. It was this festival that became the Olympic Games in 776 B. C. But they were ended in A. D. 394 by the Roman Emperor who ruled Greece. No Olympic Games were held for more than 1,500 years. Then the modern Olympics began in 1896. Almost 300 male athletes competed in the first modern Olympics. In the games held in 1900, female athletes were allowed to compete. The games have continued every four years since 1896 except during World War II, and they will most likely continue for many years to come.

Pattern Three：*Comparison*

The author explains how two or more things are alike and/or how they are different.

Sample Passage

The modern Olympics is very unlike the ancient Olympic Games. Individual events are different. While there were no swimming races in the ancient games, for example, there were chariot races. There were no female contestants and all athletes competed in the nude. Of course, the ancient and modern Olympics are also alike in many ways. Some events, such as the javelin and discus throws, are the same. Some people say that cheating, professionalism, and nationalism in the modern games are a disgrace to the Olympic tradition. But according to the ancient Greek writers, there were many cases of cheating, nationalism, and professionalism in their Olympics too.

Pattern Four: *Cause and Effect*

The author lists one or more causes and the resulting effect or effects.

Sample Passage

There are several reasons why so many people attend the Olympic Games or watch them on television. One reason is tradition. The name Olympics and the torch and flame remind people of the ancient games. People can escape the ordinariness of daily life by attending or watching the Olympics. They like to identify with someone else's individual sacrifice and accomplishment. National pride is another reason, and an athlete's or a team's hard-earned victory becomes a nation's victory. There are national medal counts and people keep track of how many medals their country's athletes have won.

Pattern Five: *Problem and Solution*

The author states a problem and lists one or more solutions to the problem. A variation of this pattern is the question-and-answer format in which the author poses a question and then answers it.

Sample Passage

One problem with modern Olympics is that it has become very big and expensive to operate. The city or country that hosts the games often loses a lot of money. A stadium, pools, and playing fields must be built for the athletic events and housing is needed for the athletes who come from around the world. And all of these facilities are used for only 2 weeks! In 1984, Los Angeles solved these problems by charging a fee for companies who wanted to be official sponsors of the games. Companies like McDonald's paid a lot of money to be part of the Olympics. Many buildings that were already built in the Los Angeles area were also used. The Coliseum where the 1932 games were held was used again and many colleges and universities in the area became playing and living sites.

Section **T**wo: Structure of Expository Writing

Topic Sentence

When you write an introduction to the expository composition, you are expected to develop a qualified topic sentence—a topic sentence with a well chosen controlling idea. If the topic sentence is too general, you will have trouble providing the necessary support. If the topic sentence is too specific, you will have difficulty in further developing it in the body. Thus, before you consider how to develop your paragraph you should (1) decide exactly what subject you are going to discuss, (2) decide on some clear stand or attitude toward your subject, and (3) write down your topic sentence (subject + attitude) in the clearest and simplest words possible.

Look at the following topic sentences:

- **Moving was a real experience for him.**
- **Moving to a new place altered his way of life.**
- **When the family moved to a larger farm, John had to start doing a man's work.**

Which of these is the most specific?

Why are the other two faulty as topic sentences?

What are the key words in Sentence Three?

With Sentence Three as a topic sentence, what would you expect the paragraph to explain?

What kind of examples might be used to support this topic sentence?

Now suppose that the writer had chosen different wording:

When his parents decided to move to another farm, John's childhood abruptly came to an end.

What are the key words in this topic sentence?

How would this topic sentence alter the emphasis of the paragraph?

What kind of examples might be used to support this topic sentence?

Again, suppose that the writer had changed the wording of the topic sentence to:

His family's move to a larger farm meant that John could no longer enjoy the carefree childhood he had shared with his brothers and sisters.

Even though each topic sentence deals with the same basic event, each new wording of the topic sentence would call for somewhat different development. This brings you to one of the qualities of the topic sentence that has been discussed previously: the topic sentence tends to establish the kind of development the writer will use.

The Body

Right from the first word, you need to consider the information that is available to you in developing your paragraph. To be adequately developed, the body of the paragraph must offer the reader everything that is promised or implied by the topic sentence, leaving no loose ends or unanswered questions.

Develop the Body with Concrete Examples

Sample Passage

Worrying

There are at least two precipitating causes of anxiety: conflict and stress. As an example of the former, we can rarely predict the precise consequences of what we do, but we are blessed (or cursed) with the intellectual capacity to anticipate the advantages and disadvantages which may accrue from any action we may be contemplating. Very commonly we are faced with a choice between several courses of action, all of which have pros and cons. This state of affairs—in psychological jargon, multiple approach-avoidance conflict— accounts for a great deal of our worrying: worrying, that is, about what to do.

The other major source of worry is the dreadful things which may happen or have happened to those we care for. Among the most stressful of these are death, illness, loss of work, money problems, marital problems and retirement. Such worries have a rational basis, but we are curiously irrational in the way we pursue them. For example, fear of death is as strong among young adults as among the elderly and it does not seem to be reduced by any sort of religious faith, including the belief that there is life after death. It is equally surprising that objective measures of anxiety suggest that we are as worried the hour before having a tooth filled as when we face major surgery.

It is difficult to decide at what point worrying stops to be "normal," but it is clearly reasonable to worry. People get seriously ill, plans go wrong, tube trains sometimes crash, etc. In fact, anxiety is judged to be pathological when it weakens our ability to live a normal life. We can manage perfectly well without traveling in planes, and an evening out isn't made uninteresting by the fact that we are unable to leave the house without checking the front door lock again and again. Such worries are wide spread in the general population.

In its extreme form, anxiety may be experienced either as a generalized, "free-floating" state(the sufferer becomes tense and frightened for no clear reason), or it may be more specifically focused—for example, on open spaces, enclosed situations or certain insects or animals. Many people will have experienced the former.

But at less intense levels, anxiety and worrying have great value. They help us to avoid trouble, or to cope with it when it cannot be avoided. Worrying may be an internal impulse, allowing us to solve problems at times of danger. It may also be an important part in helping us to come to terms with reality. In everyday life, anxiety energizes us and improves performance of many tasks, and it also helps us to achieve more, so worrying is not after all an unproductive activity. Perhaps the time to be worried is when you're not worrying.

Develop the Body with Relevant Examples

Sample Passage

Language Is a Living Thing

Language is, and should be, a living thing, constantly enriched with new words and forms of expression. But there is a vital distinction between good developments, which add to the language, enabling us to say things we could not say before, and bad developments, which subtract from the language by rendering it less precise. A vivacious, colorful use of words is not to be confused with mere slovenliness. The kind of slovenliness in which some professionals deliberately indulge is perhaps akin to the cult of the unfinished work, which has eroded most of the arts in our time. And the true answer to it is the same that art is enhanced, not hindered, by discipline. You cannot carve satisfactorily in butter.

The corruption of written English has been accompanied by an even sharper decline in the standard of spoken English. We speak very much less well than was common among educated Englishmen generation or two ago.

The modern theatre has played a baneful part in dimming our appreciation of language. Instead of the immensely articulate dialogue of, for example, Shaw (who was also very insistent off good pronunciation), audiences are now subjected to streams of barely literate trivia, often designed, only too well, to exhibit "lack of communication," and larded with the obscenities and grammatical errors of the intellectually impoverished. Emily Post once advised her readers: "The theatre is the best possible place to hear correctly-enunciated speech." Alas, no more. One young actress was recently reported to be taking lessons in how to speak badly, so that she should fit in better.

But the BBC is the worst traitor. After years of very successfully helping to raise the general standard of spoken English, it suddenly went into reverse. As the head of the pronunciation unit coyly put it: "In the 1960s the BBC opened the field to a much wider range of speakers. " To hear a BBC disc jockey talking to the latest ape-like pop idol is a truly shocking experience of verbal squalor. And the prospect seems to be of even worse to come. School teachers are actively encouraged to ignore little Johnnys incoherent grammar, atrocious spelling and haphazard punctuation, because worrying about such things might inhibit his creative genius.

Before prospective parents decide on the new baby's name, they should consider several important factors that could have an impact on their child as he or she grows older. For instance, names without specific gender such as Robin, Kelly and Chris, create confusion for teachers who are trying to schedule boy's and girl's gym classes. Master Robin is likely to find himself in the girl's gymnastic program, and Miss Kelly is likely to be named to monitor the boy's rest room. Another problem to the growing child is the fine, old family name that other children can distort in name-calling or teasing, Cosmos, Angel or Elmer. Name that would seem perfectly suitable for a newborn child is ludicrous when the child is fifty years old. Bambi may seem to be a darling name for a newborn, but Grandma Bambi is an incongruous image. Name usually associated with notorious or outrageous persons should be avoided; Adolph Hitler Smith would spend most of his life defending himself from the abuse of his peers and the disapproval of society. A child who was given a common name that is spelled differently will spend countless hours throughout life correcting report cards, registration forms, and anyone who asks his or her name for official forms. Mari, Alyce, Jonn, and Tym are examples of common names spelled uncommonly. Prospective parents should remember that of all the things they give their children, the only thing they will keep all their lives is a first name. Accordingly, the greatest care should be taken when choosing a name for a baby.

Develop the Body with Sufficient Examples

Sample Passage

Pronouncing Foreign Languages

Pronouncing a language is a skill. Every normal person is expert in the skill of pronouncing his own language; but few people are even moderately proficient at pronouncing foreign languages. Now there are many reasons for this, some obvious, some perhaps not so obvious. But I suggest that the fundamental reason why people in general do not speak foreign languages very much better than they do is that they fail to grasp the true nature of the problem of learning to pronounce, and consequently never set about tackling it in the right way. Far too many people fail to realize that pronouncing a foreign language is a skill—one that needs careful training of a special kind, and one that cannot be acquired by just leaving it to take care of itself. I think even teachers of language, while recognizing the importance of good accent, tend to neglect, in their practical teaching, the branch of study concerned with speaking the language. So the first point I want to make is that English pronunciation must be taught; the teacher should be prepared to devote some of the lesson time to this, and by his whole attitude to the subject should get the student feel that there is a matter worthy of receiving his close attention. So, there should be occasions when other aspects of English, such as grammar or spelling, are allowed for the moment to take second place.

Apart from this question of the time given to pronunciation, there are two other requirements for the teacher: first, knowledge; second, technique.

It is important that the teacher should be in possession of the necessary information. This can generally be obtained from books. It is possible to get from books some ideas of the mechanics of speech, and of what we call general phonetic theory. It is also possible in this way to get a clear mental picture of the relationship between the sounds of different languages, between the speech habits of English people and those, say, of your students. Unless the teacher has such a picture, any comments he may make on his students pronunciation are unlikely to be of much use, and lesson time spent on pronunciation may well be time wasted.

But it does not follow that you can teach pronunciation successfully as soon as you have read the necessary books. It depends, after that, on what use you make of your knowledge; and this is a matter of technique.

Now the first and most important part of a language teacher's technique is his own performance, his ability to show off the spoken language, in every detail of sound as well as in fluent speaking, so that the student's ability for imitation is given the fullest space and encouragement. The teacher, then, should be as perfect a model in this field as he can make himself. And to make his own performance better, however satisfactory this may be, the modern teacher has in his hand recordings and a radio, to supply the real voices of native speakers, or, if the teacher happens to be a native speaker himself, or speaks just like one, then to change the method of presenting the language material.

However, the process of showing pronunciation, whether by personal examples or with the help of machines, is only the beginning of teaching pronunciation. The technique of teaching each sound also needs to be considered.

The Conclusion

A paragraph that explains needs a good conclusion, but it should not end with an example. You begin with a controlling idea, provide examples to clarify it, and then conclude in a way that implies, "look reader, now that I have explained everything to you, you should be convinced that I know what I am talking about." Try to be a bit more subtle, however; a restatement of your controlling idea, once it has been fully explained, will accomplish the same purpose. It will remind your reader of the main idea and summarize the examples you have given.

Sample Passage

A reputation that took years to build can be destroyed in minutes. A man has devoted forty years of his life to his job in a bank. He has given faithful and loyal service. One day he takes two hundred dollars of the bank's money home. The man is branded a crook, an embezzler. He is fired from his job; he is forever disgraced, and possibly threatened with prison. Who remembers the forty years of good service? Again, a man who is a loving husband and a kind and provident father for twenty-five years becomes infatuated with a girl he takes out. When his wife and children learn of this, he becomes an outcast. The twenty-five good years are forgotten. A spectacular case of more than sixty years ago proves that one misstep can blast forever a carefully built reputation. In the years following World War I, the national craze for baseball grew wilder and wilder. Fans crowded into stadiums. Stars swelled into heroes. Of all the teams, the Chicago White Sox were the best with the best pitchers, runners and teamwork. Then, in 1919, the Sox threw the World Series. People took their baseball very seriously in those days, so this crookedness gave them an ugly shock. After the scandal hearings, the guilty players were too frightened of mobs to leave the courtrooms. One of the guilty players, considered the best before Babe Ruth, was Shoeless Joe Jackson. As Jackson left the hearing, a youngster called out to him, "Say it ain't so, Joe." Even though the remark has remained as a wistful part of the American language, the scandal was, unfortunately, true. The Sox were wiped out as a team and the individual members barred from organized baseball and the baseball Hall of Fame. Baseball itself came perilously close to extinction. Reputation is, indeed, a fragile thing. It takes years to build but only a moment to lose.

Section Three: Features of Expositive Essay

Expository essays require that the writer give information, explain the topic or define something. To accomplish that, they are best developed by the use of facts and statistical information, cause and effect relationships, or examples.

Expository essays also have a distinct format.

The thesis statement must be defined and narrow enough to be supported within the essay.

Each supporting paragraph must have a distinct controlling topic and all other sentences must factually relate directly to it. The transition words or phrases are important as they help the reader follow along and reinforce the logic.

Finally, the conclusion paragraph should originally restate the thesis and the main supporting ideas. Finish with a statement that reinforces your position in a meaningful and memorable way.

Never introduce new material in the conclusion.

Mini-task: *Writing Practice*

Directions: Write an essay of around 250 words on the topic "Students Should Be More Interested in the Process of Learning Than in the Facts Learned" You are required to perform the following tasks: Explain what you think of the above statement means. Describe a specific situation in which students might be more interested in the facts learned than in the process of learning. Discuss what you think determines when students should be interested in the process of learning and when they should be interested in the facts learned.

Homework

Task One: Reading and Response

Directions: Read the following passages and analyze the writing skills. You are expected to prepare a five-minute presentation on the writing skills in any of the passages and report to the whole class.

Passage One

How Men and Women Think

By Nicolas Wade

The human brain, according to an emerging new body of scientific research, comes in two different varieties, maybe as different as the accompanying physique. Men, when they are lost, instinctually fall back on their in-built navigational skills, honed from far-off days of tracking large prey miles from home. Women, by contrast, tend to find their way by the simpler methods of remembering local landmarks or even asking help from strangers.

Men excel on psychological tests that require the imaginary twisting in space of a three-dimensional object. The skill seems to help with higher math, where the topmost ranks are thronged with male minds like Andrew Wiles of Princeton, who proclaimed almost a year ago that he had proved Fermat's Last Theorem and will surely get around to publishing the proof almost any day now.

Some feminist ideologues assert that all minds are created equal and women would be just as good at math if they weren't discouraged in school. But Camilla Benbow, a psychologist at Iowa State University, has spent years assessing biases like male math teachers or parents who favor boys. She concludes that boys' superiority at math is mostly innate.

But women, the new studies assert, have the edge in most other ways, like perceptual speed, verbal fluency and communication skills. They also have sharper hearing than men, and excel in taste, smell and touch, and in fine coordination of hand and eye. If Martians arrived and gave job interviews, it seems likely they would direct men to competitive sports and manual labor and staff most professions, diplomacy and government with women.

The measurement of intellectual differences is a field with a long and mostly disgraceful past. I. Q. tests have been regularly misused, sometimes even concocted, in support of prevailing prejudices. Distinguished male anatomists used to argue that women were less intelligent because their brains weighed less, neglecting to correct for the strong influence of body weight on brain weight.

The present studies of sex differences are venturing on ground where self-deception and prejudice are constant dangers. The science is difficult and the results prone to misinterpretation. Still, the budding science seems free so far of obvious error. For one thing, many of the field's leading practitioners happen to be women, perhaps because male academics in this controversial field have had their lives made miserable by militant feminists.

For another, the study of brain sex differences does not depend on just one kind of subvertible measure but draws on several different disciplines, including biology and anatomy. As is described in a new book, *Eve's Rib*, by Robert Pool, and the earlier *Brain Sex*, by Anne Moir and David Jessel, the foundations of the field have been carefully laid in animal research. Experiments with rats show that exposure in the womb to testosterone indelibly imprints a male pattern of behavior; without testosterone, the rat's brain is female.

In human fetuses, too, the sex hormones seem to mold a male and female version of the brain, each subtly different in organization and behavior. The best evidence comes from girls with a rare genetic anomaly who are exposed in the womb to more testosterone than normal; they grow up doing better than their unaffected sisters on the tests that boys are typically good at. There's also some evidence, not yet confirmed, that male and female brains may be somewhat differently structured, with the two cerebral hemispheres being more specialized and less well interconnected in men than in women.

If the human brain exists in male and female versions, as modulated in the womb, that would explain what every parent knows, that boys and girls prefer different patterns of play regardless of well-meaning efforts to impose unisex toys on both.

The human mind being very versatile, however, any genetic propensities are far from decisive. In math, for example, the average girl is pretty much as good as the average boy. Only among the few students at the peak of math ability do boys predominate. Within the loose framework set by the genes, education makes an enormous difference. In Japan, boys exceed girls on the mental rotation tests, just as in the United States. But the Japanese girls outscore American boys. Maybe Japanese kids are just smarter or, more likely, just better taught, Japan being a country where education is taken seriously and parents and teachers consistently push children to excel.

There are some obvious cautions to draw about the social and political implications that might one day flow from brain sex research. One is that differences between individuals of the same sex often far exceed the slight differences between the sexes as two population groups: "If I were going into combat, I would prefer to have Martina Navratilova at my side than Robert Reich," says Patricia Ireland, president of the National Organization for Women. Even if men in general excel in math, an individual woman could still be better than most men.

On the other hand, if the brains of men and women really are organized differently, it's possible the sexes both prefer and excel at different occupations, perhaps those with more or less competition or social interaction. "In a world of scrupulous gender equality, equal numbers of girls and boys would be educated and trained for... all the professions... [Hiring would proceed] until half of every workplace was made up of men and half, women," says Judith Lorber in *Paradoxes of Gender*, a new work of feminist theory. That premise does not hold if there are real intellectual differences between the sexes; the test of equal opportunity, when all unfair barriers to women have fallen, will not necessarily be equal outcomes.

Greek mythology tells that Tiresias, having lived both as a man and a woman for some complicated reason, was asked to settle a dispute between Zeus and Hera as to which gender enjoyed sex more. He replied there was no contest—it was 10 times better for women. Whereupon Hera struck him blind for his insolence and Zeus in compensation gave him the gift of foresight. Like Tiresias, the brain sex researchers are uncovering some impolitic truths, potent enough to shake Mount Olympus some day.

Passage Two

"There" Is No Better than "Here"

By Cherie Cater-Scott

Many people believe that they will be happy once they arrive at some specific goal they set for themselves. However, more often than not, once you arrive "there" you will still feel dissatisfied, and move your "there" vision to yet another point in the future. By always chasing after another "there," you are never really appreciating what you already have right "here." It is important for human beings to keep sober minded about the age-old drive to look beyond the place where you now stand. On one hand, your life is enhanced by your dreams and aspirations. On the other hand, these drives can pull you farther and farther from your enjoyment of your life right now. By learning the lessons of gratitude and abundance, you can bring yourself closer to fulfilling the challenge of living in the present.

Gratitude To be grateful means you are thankful for and appreciative of what you have and where you are on your path right now. Gratitude fills your heart with the joyful feeling and allows you to fully appreciate everything that arises on your path. As you strive to keep your focus on the present moment, you can experience the full wonder of "here."

There are many ways to cultivate gratitude. Here are just a few suggestions you may wish to try:

1. Imagine what your life would be like if you lost all that you had. This will most surely remind you of how much you do appreciate it.

2. Make a list each day of all that you are grateful for, so that you can stay conscious

daily of your blessings. Do this especially when you are feeling as though you have nothing to feel grateful for. Or spend a few minutes before you go to sleep giving thanks for all that you have.

3. Spend time offering assistance to those who are less fortunate than you, so that you may gain perspective.

However you choose to learn gratitude is irrelevant. What really matters is that you create a space in your consciousness for appreciation for all that you have right now, so that you may live more joyously in your present moment.

Abundance　One of the most common human fears is scarcity. Many people are afraid of not having enough of what they need or want, and so they are always striving to get to a point when they would finally have enough.

Alan and Linda always dreamed of living "the good life." Both from poor working-class families, they married young and set out to fulfill their mutual goal of becoming wealthy. They both worked very hard for years, amassing a small fortune, so they could move from their two-bedroom home to a palatial seven-bedroom home in the most upscale neighborhood. They focused their energies on accumulating all the things they believed signified abundance: membership in the local exclusive country club, luxury cars, designer clothing, and high-class society friends. No matter how much they accumulated; however, it never seemed to be enough. They were unable to erase the deep fear of scarcity both had acquired in childhood. They needed to learn the lesson of abundance. Then the stock market crashed in 1987, and Alan and Linda lost a considerable amount of money. A bizarre but costly lawsuit depleted another huge portion of their savings. One thing led to another, and they found themselves in a financial disaster. Assets needed to be sold, and eventually they lost the country club membership, the cars, and the house. It took several years and much hard work for Alan and Linda to land on their feet, and though they now live a life far from extravagant, they have taken stock of their lives and feel quite blessed. Only now, as they assess what they have left—a solid, loving marriage, their health, a dependable income, and good friends—do they realize that true abundance comes not from amassing, but rather from appreciating.

Scarcity consciousness arises as a result of the "hole-in-the-soul syndrome." This is when we attempt to fill the gaps in our inner lives with things from the outside world. But like puzzle pieces, you can't fit something in where it does not naturally belong. No amount of external objects, affection, love, or attention can ever fill an inner void. We already have enough, so we should revel in our own interior abundance.

Passage Three

Youth

By Samuel Ullman

Youth is not a time of life; it is a state of mind; it is not a matter of rosy cheeks, red lips and supple knees; it is a matter of the will, a quality of the imagination, a vigor of the emotions; it is the freshness of the deep springs of life.

Youth means a tempera-mental predominance of courage over timidity, of the appetite for adventure over the love of ease. This often exists in a man of 60 more than a boy of 20. Nobody grows old merely by a number of years. We grow old by deserting our ideals.

Years may wrinkle the skin, but to give up enthusiasm wrinkles the soul. Worry, fear, self-distrust bows the heart and turns the spring back to dust.

Whether 60 or 16, there is in every human being's heart the lure of wonder, the unfailing childlike appetite of what's next and the joy of the game of living. In the center of your heart and my heart there is a wireless station: so long as it receives messages of beauty, hope, cheer, courage and power from men and from the Infinite, so long are you young.

When the aerials are down, and your spirit is covered with snows of cynicism and the ice of pessimism, then you are grown old, even at 20, but as long as your aerials are up, to catch waves of optimism, there is hope you may die young at 80.

Unit Thirteen
Résumé and Cover Letter

第十三单元　求职简历

要点提示：求职简历是对个人学历、工作经历或能力的客观陈述，其目的是争取面试的机会。求职简历应长短适度，以一页为宜；应详略得当，重点突出；应使招聘者在读"历史"的基础上发掘应聘者未来的潜质。求职简历的内容一般包括：详细联系方式、工作目标设置、学历、工作经历、工作绩效、特长等。内容编排的先后可灵活变更，但布局应美观大方、清晰明了。

Introductory Remarks

A résumé is a brief record of one's personal history and qualifications that is typically prepared by an applicant for a job. Although recruiters sometimes refer to the résumé as what one has learned or done, the emphasis of the résumé should be on the future rather than the past: you must show how your education and work experience have prepared you for future jobs—specifically the job for which you are applying.

Right from the start, be realistic about the purpose of your résumé. Few people are actually hired on the basis of their résumé alone (However, many people are not hired because of their poorly written or poorly presented résumé). Instead, applicants are generally hired on the basis of their performance during a job interview.

Thus, the purpose of the résumé is to get you an interview, and the purpose of the interview is to get you a job. Remember, however, that the résumé and accompanying application letter (cover letter) are crucial in advancing you beyond the mass of applicants and into the much smaller group of potential candidates invited to an interview.

Warm-Up Exercises

Exercise One

Directions: Read the following résumé and make comments on its format, length, and contents.

Patricia L. Bailey

112 Campus Drive, Apt. B

Bloomington, IN 47401

Phone: 812-555-9331

Job Objective

   Professional position in hotel management in the Chicago metropolitan area

Education

   Bachelor of Science in Business Administration, Indiana University, May 2004

   Major: Hospitality Services Administration

   Minor: Marketing

- Achieved overall grade-point average of 3.4 (on a 4.0 scale)
- Received Board of Regents' scholarship
- Financed 75% of college expenses through savings and part-time work

Work Experience

   Assistant Manager, McDonald's Restaurant, Bloomington, Indiana

   2001-Present (full-time during summer; part-time during school year)

- Advanced to this position after only six months as a counter clerk
- Developed work schedules for 23 part-time employees
- Designed and administered several successful employer incentive projects
- Gained considerable practical experience in supervising employees and handling human-relation problems

   Student Intern, Valley Hideaway, South Bend, Indiana

September-December 2003 / Full-time internship sponsored by Indiana University

- Worked as the assistant to the night manager of a 200-room resort
- Gained experience in operating the Guest Service management system
- Was responsible for producing daily and weekly occupancy reports

Personal Data

Active member of Sigma Iota Epsilon (business honor society)

Treasurer of Hospitality Service Association

Reference Available Upon Request

Exercise Two: *Small Group Discussion*

Directions: Discuss in small groups the purpose, the length, the format, and the content of a résumé.

Exercise Three: *Report Presentation*

Directions: Each group has one representative to report its discussion.

Introduction to Résumé Writing

Section One: Length

Decisions about résumé length become much easier when you consider what happens on the receiving end: recruiters typically spend no more than 35 seconds looking at each résumé during their initial screening to pare down the perhaps hundreds of applicants for a position into a manageable number to study in more detail. How much information can the recruiters be expected to read in less than a minute? It won't matter how qualified you are if no one ever reviews those qualifications.

How much is appropriate? Surveys of employment and human resource executives consistently show that most managers prefer a one-page résumé for the entry-level positions typically sought by recent college graduates, with a two-page résumé being reserved for unusual circumstances or for higher-level positions.

According to one survey of 200 executives from major U. S. firms, the most serious mistake job candidates make is including too much information in their résumé. Their ranking (in percentages of the whole) of the most serious résumé errors is as follows:

Too long	32%
Grammatical errors	25%
No descriptions of job functions	18%
Unprofessional appearance	15%
Achievements omitted	10%
	100%

A one-page résumé is not the same as a two-page résumé crammed onto one page by means of small type and narrow margins. Your résumé must be attractive and easy to read. Shorten your résumé by making judicious decisions about what to include and then by using concise language to communicate what is important.

Do not, on the other hand, make your résumé too short. A résumé that does not fill one page may tell the prospective employer that you have little to offer. It has been estimated that one page is ideal for 85% of all résumés, and that is the length you should target.

Section Two: Format

Although the content of your résumé is obviously more important than the format, remember that first impressions are important. As pointed out earlier, those first impressions are formed during the half-minute that is typically devoted to the initial screening of each résumé. Therefore, even before you begin writing your résumé, think about the format, because some format decisions will affect the amount of space available to discuss your qualifications and background.

If you prepare your résumé and application letter on a computer, you can easily customize them for each employment opportunity. In addition, you'll be sending the employer a nonverbal message that you know how to use a computer and word processing software.

Choose a simple, easy-to-read typeface, and avoid the temptation to use a lot of "special effects" just because they're available on your computer. One or two typefaces in one or two different sizes should be enough. Use a simple format with lots of white space, short paragraphs, and a logical organization. Type your résumé, and arrange it in an attractive, easy-to-read format.

Section Three: Content

Fortunately, perhaps, there is no such thing as a standard résumé; each is as individual as the person it represents. There are, however, standard parts of the résumé—those parts recruiters expect and need to see to make valid judgments. For example, one survey of 152 Fortune 500 company personnel indicated that 90% or more wanted the following information on a résumé:

- Name, address, and telephone number
- Job objective
- College major, degree, name of college, and date of graduation
- Jobs held, employing company or companies, date of employment, and job duties
- Special aptitudes and skills

Identifying Information

It doesn't do any good to impress a recruiter if he or she cannot contact you easily to schedule an interview; therefore, your name and complete address (including phone number) are crucial.

Your name should be the very first item on the résumé, arranged attractively at the top. Use whatever form you typically use for signing your name. Give your complete name, avoiding nicknames, and do not use a personal title such as Mr. or Ms.

Increasingly, employers are also expecting an e-mail address to be listed. An e-mail address not only provides another means of contact but also sends a non-verbal message that you are computer savvy.

Job Objective

The job objective is a short summary of your area of expertise and career interest. As indicated, most recruiters want the objective stated so that they will know where you might fit into their organization.

Don't force the employer to guess about your career goals.

Don't waste the objective's prominent spot at the top of your résumé by giving a weak, over-general goal.

For your objective to help you, it must be personalized both for you and for the position you are seeking. Also, it must be specific enough to be useful to the prospective employer but not so specific as to exclude you from possible positions.

Mini-task: *Pair Work*

Directions: Work in pairs to discuss the following job objectives to see whether they meet the above-mentioned job objective criteria.

- "A paid, one-semester internship in marketing or advertising"
- "Position in personal sales in a medium-sized manufacturing firm"
- "Opportunity to apply my accounting education and English-language skill in a joint venture"
- "A public relations position requiring well-developed communication, administrative, and computer skills"
- "To gain the experience of teaching in Chinese culture"
- "A position that offers both a challenge and an opportunity for growth"
- "A challenging position in a progressive organization"
- "A responsible position that lets me use my education and experience and that provides opportunities for increased responsibilities"
- "A position reporting to the Board"

Education

Unless your work experience has been extensive, fairly high level, and directly related to your job objective, your education is probably a stronger job qualification than your work experience and should therefore come first on the résumé.

List the name of your college, and its location if needed, your major and minor, and your expected date of graduation (month and year).

List your grade-point average if it will set you apart from the competition. If you have made the dean's list or have financed any substantial portion of your college expenses through part-time work or scholarships, mention that. Unless your course of study provided distinctive experiences that uniquely qualify you for the job, avoid including a lengthy list of college courses.

Working Experience

Today, an increasing number of college students in China have some work experience to bring to their future jobs. Work experience—any work experience—is a definite plus. It shows the employer that you have had experience in satisfying a superior, following directions, accomplishing objectives through group work, and being rewarded for your work. If your work experience has been directly related to your job objective, consider putting it ahead of the education section, where it will receive more emphasis.

When relating your work experience, use either a chronological or functional organizational pattern.

- Chronological: In a chronological arrangement, you organize your experience by date, describing your most recent job first and working backward. This format is most appropriate when you have had a strong continuing work history and much of your work has been related to your job objective. About 95% of all résumés are chronological, beginning with the most recent information and working backward.
- Functional: In a functional arrangement, you organize your experience by type of function performed (such as supervision or budgeting) or skill developed (such as human relations or communication skills). Functional résumés are most appropriate when you are changing industries, moving into an entirely different line of work, or reentering the work force after a long period of unemployment, because they emphasize your skills rather than your employment history and let you show how these skills have broad applicability to other jobs.

Show how your work experience qualifies you for the type of job which you are applying for. Highlight those transferable skills:

- ability to work well with others
- communication skills
- competence and good judgment
- innovation
- high-level computer proficiency
- reliability and trustworthiness
- enthusiasm
- honest and moral character
- increasing responsibility

Other Relevant Information

If you have special skills that might give you an edge over the competition, (such as knowledge of a foreign language and computer proficiency), list them.

Include any honors or recognitions that have relevance to the job you are seeking.

Other optional information includes hobbies, travel experiences, willingness to travel, and health status. Such information may be included if it has direct relevance to your desired job and if you have room for it, but it may be safely omitted if you need space for more important information.

Section Four: Wording Skills for Résumé Writing

Use Concrete, Achievement-Oriented Words to Describe Your Experience

Start your descriptions with action verbs, using present tense for current duties and past tense for previous job duties or accomplishments (complete sentences are not necessary). Concrete words such as the following make your work experience come alive:

accomplished	designed	operated
achieved	determined	administered
developed	organized	applied
directed	planned	approved
prepared	arranged	established
presented	assisted	evaluated
presided	authorized	forecast
produced	balanced	generated
purchased	budgeted	guided
recommended	built	handled
reported	changed	hired
researched	collected	implemented
revised	communicated	increased
scheduled	completed	instituted

screened	conceived	interviewed
introduced	simplified	conducted
investigated	concluded	consolidated
led	studied	constructed
maintained	supervised	contracted
marketed	trained	managed
controlled	coordinated	modified
transformed	created	motivated
updated	delegated	negotiated

Avoid weak verbs such as attempted, endeavored, hoped, and tried. When possible, ensure credibility by listing specific accomplishment, giving numbers or amounts. Highlight especially those accomplishments that have direct relevance to the desired job. Here are some examples:

Not: I was responsible for a large sales territory.

But: Managed a six-country sales territory; increased sales 13% during first full year.

Not: I worked as a clerk in the cashier's office.

But: Balanced the case register every day; was the only part-time employee entrusted to make nightly cash deposits.

Mini-task: *Writing*

Directions: Write a résumé based on the wanted advertisement given below.

Era, a Shantou-based company, is one of the largest companies producing black and white films and X-ray papers in China. We would like to invite highly-talented candidates to join our team for achieving our company objectives. Reporting to the Board, you will be responsible for setting up the company's overall strategies, carrying out market research, designing products as well as managing the operations of branch offices in Guangzhou, Beijing, and Shanghai. You are also expected to establish, develop, and maintain excellent relationships with agents, carriers, customers, as well as governmental departments.

Section Five: Cover Letter

A cover letter is a letter of introduction to an employer. The purpose of a cover letter is to obtain an interview, not to tell a lengthy story. Therefore, a cover letter should be simple, clear and focused on your qualifications closely related to the job you are applying for.

Content of a Cover Letter

Paragraph One: tell the addressee when, where, from whom you got the inviting information and state your purpose of writing this specific cover letter.

Paragraph Two: explain why you believe that you are the right person for the position you are applying for.

Paragraph Three: draw a natural conclusion based on previous explanation and offer contact information.

Types of Cover Letter

Generally, cover letters can be classified into two categories—specific and general. The specific cover letter is directed at a specific firm, a specific person, and a specific position. The specific cover letter personally addresses the needs of the firm and sends a positive message to the employer that you are truly interested in and qualified for the position you are applying for. While a general cover letter is often addressed Dear Employer, and stresses your qualifications in hope that a position will be available to utilize your skills. A general cover letter does not direct at a specific company, a specific person, or a specific position, but offers your qualifications for potential employers.

Sample Cover Letters

SALLY B. DOE
7124 S. Decoto Street
Any Town, Any State 36254
Telephone: (815) 879-2680
January 30, 2009

Mr. Smith—Dir. of Human Resources
Raymond Kate Associates
524 Fair Lane Street
Any City, State 78194

Dear Mr. Smith:

I am responding to your advertisement in *The City Tribune* (dated Jan. 20, 2008), regarding the Pharmaceutical Representative position. Please find enclosed my résumé showing my education, experience, and background.

I have over 7-year experience in the sales and marketing field, and 3-year experience as an LPN staff nurse.

Throughout my sales and marketing career I won top sales awards, and trained other sales representative specific sales techniques to increase their sales. I enjoy working with the public, as well, demonstrating products, and educating others in their uses. I believe I would excel in pharmaceutical sales because I truly find sales a challenging and rewarding career; my nursing background offers an advantage in better understanding the products I would sell.

May you arrange an interview to further discuss my qualifications? I am available for an interview at a mutually convenient time.

Thank you for your time and consideration.

Sincerely,

Sally B. Doe

BILL J. DOE

942 Sunset Circle

Hampton, Virginia 84217

(555) 555-0000

Dear Employer:

In response to your advertisement regarding the safety/loss control position in your organization, I am enclosing a résumé for your review. Please consider this letter as my formal application presenting my background, education and experience.

I have over 8-year experience in the Health and Safety field; and I am well versed in Health and Safety issues in conjunction with state and federal guidelines.

I have considerable experience in dealing with insurance claims and litigation; and a thorough knowledge of the process and procedures of the corporate environment. I work well with people and enjoy getting the work at hand completed.

Below is a list of agencies I have extensive consulting experience with:

Virginia Workers Compensation Commission—Environmental Protection Agency—

Occupational Health and Safety Administration—Department of Transportation—Virginia Natural Resources Conservation Commission—Federal Aviation Administration.

May you arrange an interview to further discuss my qualifications? I am available for an interview at a mutually convenient time.

Thank you for your time and consideration.

Salary History:

Planned Health Care, Inc. $38,000.00

Jonet Group, Inc. $25,750.00

City of Millington $18,000.00

Sincerely,

Bill J. Doe

Encl.

Homework

Task One: Writing

Directions: Write a comparison and contrast composition on the similarities and differences between Chinese and English résumés. You need to include the following information in your composition:

- similarities between the two
- differences between the two
- possible causes for the differences
- Which one do you prefer? Give reasons.

Task Two: Reading

Directions: Read the passages given below and summarize the main idea of each passage respectively.

Passage One

Résumé Objective

There are differing opinions on the relevance of stating your objective at the beginning of your résumé. Some people feel it is entirely irrelevant, however we disagree.

A résumé without an objective has no focus or sense of direction. As we have previously stated, it is vital that your résumé conveys a sense of purpose to your prospective employer.

To ensure that your prospective employer is aware of your intentions you must state an objective. State the job you are seeking. Your résumé must then revolve around this objective with one intention—to gain the position you are seeking through the correct emphasis on your skills and experience.

Your objective should be a simple statement of intent. Examples are as follows:

Objective: Seeking a position as an Administrative Assistant where extensive experience and superior organization skills will be fully utilized.

Objective: Seeking a position within Operations Management where a proven record of success will be utilized and further developed.

A statement such as this will immediately capture the interest and attention of your prospective employer.

Alternatively if you so wish you may use a general objective stating the position you seek only:

Objective: Operations Manager

Objective: Administrative Assistant

This is not used so frequently as the first example, but it is entirely appropriate. So you may choose the example that is more suited to your résumé style.

Remember the intention is to gain the interest of your prospective employer and it is the content within your résumé that must work for you.

Passage Two

A Sample Cover Letter

2244 Oak Street

Rockville, MD 20859

July 1, 2008

Ms. Joan Hirer

Director of Personnel

Imagemakers, Inc.

4000 75th Street

New York, NY 10004

Dear Ms. Hirer：

Your Personnel Job Vacancy Listing is announcing the position of Public Information Specialist in your Department of Public Relations. I am very interested in being considered for this position.

While a student at Gallaudet University, I majored in communication arts and took several courses related to public relations. I also did two internships in the public relations field through our University's co-op internship program. During my internships with the Government of the District of Colombia and with Giant Food, Inc., I answered inquiries about various services and programs and helped research and develop some materials for constituents and consumers.

Enclosed is my résumé, which contains more details about my work experience and educational accomplishments.

I am confident that I could contribute valuable ideas and skills to your organization. I would like to arrange an opportunity for us to meet and will contact you within two weeks to set up an interview. Should you or your staff wish to contact me earlier, please call me at （301）723-7543. Because I am deaf, I suggest that you call me through a relay telephone service. To do this, call （800）735-2258. The relay agent will answer your call, and call me using teletype equipment （TTY）. Then the agent will relay your comments to me, and mine to you.

I am looking forward to meeting you and sharing more about my abilities and experience.

Sincerely，

Sally Greatworker

Enclosure

（Developed by the Gallaudet University Career Center）

Unit Fourteen
Letter Writing

第十四单元 书信写作

要点提示：书信种类繁多，内涵丰富，且为生活、工作和学习所必须之交流工具，因此是英语为第二语言者提升写作能力的最有效路径之一。书信的形式、内容及结构随交际目的及对象的不同而各异，需要学习者认真领会，细加区分。又由于中英文化的差异，中英文书信在词语规范、篇章布局、内容取舍等方面均存在较大差异，这是学习英文书信写作的重点和难点，更是跨文化交际必须具备的知识基础。

Introductory Remarks

Letter writing can prove to be one of the most practical ways to engage ESL students in the writing process. ESL students can learn many of the key requirements of a typical writing class through the process of letter writing, for letter writing, just as essays writing, requires organization, clarity, a focus on word choice, and a careful attention to detail.

Another reason for us to include letter writing in this book is that there exist quite a few differences between English and Chinese letter writing. In both languages and cultures, there are specific formats that we should follow, whether in writing personal or business correspondence. Besides the formats, the content is also somewhat different. For example, in a Chinese letter of application, there is often no "job objective" stated as often found in an English cover letter. Chinese writers tend to include information that is not directly related to the job, while English writers are less likely to do so.

Warm-Up Exercise

Directions: Read the following two letters, and discuss the differences between them in small groups by focusing on the differences between formal and informal letters in formats, writing styles, wording, situations that call for a formal or informal letter, etc.

Letter One

March 3, 2012

Dear Grace,

Very sorry for responding so late, but I am glad to hear that you have access to so many interesting and informative courses at your university. Work hard and be my instructor this coming winter vacation, will you?

Our campus is pretty beautiful. It lies at the foot of a large mountain with a river flowing in front, a scenic spot where many great scholars taught or studied. We all like to do morning exercise in the woods, and have a stroll along the river bank after supper.

Life here is also rich and colorful. Although classmates are from various provinces, we get along with each other. On the weekend, we would go to the party and have a dance, or go to see a film. Sometimes, we also hold a party to practice our oral English, or go to the English Corner to have conversations with foreign instructors and other students. In a word, I deeply appreciate my life here.

Grace, how about you? Do you appreciate the feeling of a college freshman? Please tell me all about yourself whenever you can spare a few minutes.

Yours,
Portia

Letter Two

196 Park Avenue
New York, NY. 18000
May 6, 2012

Mr. John Smith
820 Boynton Avenue
Bronx, New York

Dear Mr. Smith:

I have just seen your advertisement in the *New York Times* offering to exchange English for Chinese lessons.

I am a visiting scholar from China and will be here until next July. I am female and have been teaching mathematics at Shantou University for ten years.

My English isn't too bad, but I would very much like to further improve it. The only difficulty is that I have a heavy research and teaching load and would only be free in the evenings. Maybe the best thing would be for both of us to meet sometime and have a talk to see if we can be of any help to each other.

My daytime phone number is 754-6679 and my home number is 237-8528. If I'm not available, please leave your phone number on the answer phone.

Yours truly,
Peng Yu

Section One: Formats of Letters

An English letter usually consists of six parts, i.e., heading, inside address, salutation, body, complimentary close, and signature.

Heading (**the addresser's address**): In the upper right hand corner of the first page, write your full address and the date. The heading might be unnecessary if the addressee is your close friend or relative and knows your address well.

Inside Address (**the addressee's address**): On the left side, above the salutation, put the name and full address of the addressee. However, this is often omitted in personal letters.

Salutation: The greeting to the addressee, written flush with the left margin, two spaces below the inside address. A comma (,) follows the salutation in a personal letter; in a business letter, it is followed by a colon (:). Besides, in personal letters, first names are usually used, while in business letters, the surnames are used.

Body: The message tends to be transferred or the contents covered in a letter.

Complimentary Close: it refers to the closing of a letter. The conventional complimentary closes in business letters are "Yours truly," "Yours sincerely," "Sincerely yours," "Sincerely," "Cordially yours," "Yours cordially," etc. The close of a personal letter is of a freer choice "Yours," "Affectionately," "Yours with love," "Love," "With best wishes," etc.

      Signature：Put your name（always in handwritten form）.

Section **T**wo: Types of English Letters

Type One：*A Thank-you Letter*

    A thank-you letter is also referred to as a bread-and-butter letter, which is probably the most frequently used form in our daily lives. A thank-you letter should be written whenever someone does you a favor—gives you a gift, invites you to dinner, writes a letter of recommendation for you, comes to your support unexpectedly...when you write a thank-you letter, extend your sincere expression of gratitude to the addressee at the very beginning, recall the event, express your favorable feelings, and list simply the reasons for offering your gratitude in the body, and express your wish to have the opportunity to reciprocate the past favor.

Sample

May 8, 2012

Dear Daniel,

    Thank you very much for the wonderful holiday vacation I spent with you and your family. Your mother is such a terrific cook! I think I must have gained 10 pounds in just a week I spent with you. I really appreciate your taking time off from work to take me around and show me so many places. You are lucky to live in such an interesting area. I hope that soon you will be able to visit my part of the country. Thank you again for a wonderful time. Let's keep in touch.

                                     Wish you all the best,
                                     Matthew

Type Two：*A Letter of Invitation*

    A letter of invitation is a written request sent to ask for the recipient's presence or participation in an event. It is an effective means to establish, develop and maintain relationships with other people and enhance emotional exchange. When you write a letter of invitation, state clearly your purpose of writing at the very beginning, explain the reasons for the invitation and describe the requirements as well as the details of the events in the body, and express your expectation of an early reply or confirmation from the addressee at the end of the letter.

Sample

6/F, Tin Ka Ping Building
The Chinese University of Hong Kong
Shatin, N. T. , Hong Kong
March 21, 2012

Ronald, Robertson: Professor
Department of Critical Languages
Indiana University
Indiana, PA 15701
U. S. A.

Dear Professor Robertson:

Congratulations! You are invited to attend the Fifth International Conference on Chinese Education for the 21st Century, to be held at the Chinese University of Hong Kong from August 13—19, 2012. Your paper, which was among only thirty papers selected from the 104 which were submitted for consideration, will be included in the program and will be circulated to the participants in advance.

The conference planning committee will provide your lodging and a meals allowance of HK $ 300 per day for seven days. You will be expected to provide your own transportation and to pay a registration fee of HK $ 500 (520 yuan RMB). Details regarding the formatting of your paper, the registration procedure, and other matters are included on separate sheet. Please advise as soon as possible whether or not you can accept this invitation.

Cordially yours,
David L. Angus, Co-chair
Conference Planning Committee

Type Three: *A Letter of Apology*

A letter of apology is what we write to a person or an organization to apologize for not being able to do something as requested, arranged or promised, or for the case of doing something wrong or treating someone in a wrong way. When you write a letter of apology, express your sincere apology at the very beginning, explain the situation in the body, and show your willingness to make up for it at the end.

Sample

May 4, 2012

Dear Gary,

I do want to apologize to you.

We haven't talked to each other for two months since we had an argument. I know I should not have criticized the girl you love. I should not have said she was ugly and stupid. It never occurred to me that you would yell at me and turn to leave immediately. It made me angry and I decided not to talk to you.

At first, I thought it was all your fault. Before long, you would apologize to me as you always did and then we would be reconciled. But as time went by, I calmed down and reflected on what I had done to you. I found I was too reckless to care about your feelings. Even though I had something to say, I should have expressed myself in a mild and tactful way. I know I was wrong. I would like to ask for your forgiveness. After all, a true friend is uneasy to find. I don't want to lose a good friend like you. We should cherish our friendship and try our best to keep it, right? If your answer is "Yes", please give me a smile and say "Hi" next time you see me.

Your friend,
Amy

Type Four: A Letter of Congratulation

A letter of congratulation is what we write to congratulate someone on their anniversary, birthday, wedding, promotion, or graduation. When we write a letter of congratulation, we say our best wishes early in the message and again when we close. Make sure you mention the occasion that is being celebrated. Do not add other news or information in the message, with the exception of birthday cards. Express how happy you are for the person and how you learned about the delightful news. Avoid going overboard on flattery. Be positive and pleasant. If you have an objection about an event, do not include that in your message, or do not write a letter at all.

Sample

Dear Barbara and Ken,

Congratulations on your engagement! I wish you the best and look forward to your wedding day. Thank you for your lovely invitation.

Again, warmest congratulations!

Love,

Maria G.

Type Five: A Letter of Inquiry

A letter of inquiry refers to any letter that seeks information or asks for help. When you write a letter of inquiry, you are expected to state the main idea first, give explanation and details next, and then draw a friendly close.

Sample

Heading

Inside address

Dear Mr. Gleason:

Would you please provide me with information regarding your HP340 portable printer? I'm interested in purchasing 34 lightweight printers that our marketing representatives can use with their Toshiba 1200XE notebook computer when they travel.

Specifically, I would like to know the answers to the following three questions:

1. Is the HP 340 a laser printer?

2. Is it battery operated?

3. Does it come with at least a six-month warranty?

I would appreciate your faxing me the information I need to make a purchase decision (Fax:919-555-0327). I would also appreciate receiving ordering information.

Sincerely,

Carolyn J. Ryerson, Purchasing Director

Home Security Procucts

Type Six: A Letter of Complaint

A letter of complaint is written to have something improved or a problem remedied. For example, the buyer writes a letter of complaint to the seller to complain the poor service, poor quality of the product(s), unfair practices, or the like. When you write a letter of complaint, you are supposed to introduce yourself briefly, refer to the subject of complaint, state the purpose for writing this letter, and come to a friendly close.

Sample

Dear Sir / Madam:

I am an overseas student from China, who studies in the Department of Civil Engineering. I used to be quite satisfied with the accommodation offered by you. However, recently, many unpleasant things have taken place, which cause me a lot of inconvenience and trouble. Therefore I am now writing to draw your attention to my present situation in hope that it will be kindly improved.

The most nettlesome is that many facilities in my dorm are out of order: the faucet in the toilet cannot be turned off so that the water is running all day long. Secondly, the air-conditioner breaks down. It is broiling these days. Worst of all, two weeks ago, a snack bar was opened right under my window, which has brought me endless trouble—the noise, the inviting smell and the choky smoke.

I eagerly hope that you can look into my case and improve it as soon as possible. Please send a repairman to handle my room facilities and advise the snack bar to improve its management so as to reduce its impact on the neighborhood as far as possible.

Thank you for your kind consideration. I am looking forward to your prompt and favorable reply.

Sincerely yours,
Zeng Qiliang

Type Seven: A Letter of Adjustment

A letter of adjustment is written to inform the addressee of the action taken in response to his or her letter of complaint or letter of claim. When you write a letter of adjustment, you are expected to respond promptly, tell the addressee immediately what adjustment is being made (the good news first), provide convincing and reasonable explanation and draw a positive and forward-looking closing.

Sample

April 22 , 2012

Ms. Claire Scriven
Marketing Manager
Rubbermaid Incorporated
1147 Akron Road
Wooster , Ohio 44691-6000

Dear Ms. Scriven:

Color-Vu Graphics is, of course, happy to cancel the $176.50 charge for Invoice 4073. I appreciate your taking the time to write and send us a sample slide (you may simply discard the other slides).

Upon receiving your letter, I immediately sent your slide to our quality-control personnel for closer examination. They agreed with you that the slide should have been redeveloped before it left our processing lab. We have now revised our procedures to ensure that before each slide leaves our lab, it is inspected by someone other than the person preparing it.

To better serve the media needs of our corporate customers, we are installing the Kodak 1120 processor, the most sophisticated development system available. Thus, when you send us your next order you'll see that your slides are of even higher quality than those in the Business Management advertisement that impressed you.

Sincerely yours,
David Foster
Customer Relations

Type Eight: A Letter of Application

A letter of application refers to a letter in which you express your desire to seek a position in a certain working unit. When you write a letter of application, in the beginning, you are expected to state when, where, how you got the inviting information, and your purpose in writing the letter; in the body of the letter, you are supposed to provide personal information relevant to the job you are seeking, and elaborate on your specific qualifications and ability such as your education background, your working experience, and other information expedient; at the end of the letter, express your wish for an interview, show your appreciation to the recipient for his or her favorable consideration extended to your application.

Sample

Heading

Inside address

Dear Sir / Madam：

I am quite interested in your company since the position, according to your description, sounds exactly the very kind of job I am seeking. I cherish it as a fortune and send this letter. As a famous saying goes, "Opportunity knocks, but only once." I think myself a competent candidate for the position you offered.

I major in International Trade and Economics, and will graduate from Nanjing University next June. My courses include International Trade, International Economics, International Business, International Business Negotiation, Economics, Business English, Business Oral English, and other relevant courses. I have grasped the "basics" of my major, and skills of practice as well. Besides, I am quite interested in English and computer science, and have attained a fair knowledge in these fields, as I have passed CET-6 and C Language of Level 2 of Jiangsu Province. In my extracurricular time, I devote my passion to computer skills and English, and enjoy myself with music, web designing, Flash Making, and Photoshop. I am also quite proficient in such software as the Office Series like Word, PowerPoint, Excel, etc. Bearing these in mind, I venture the opinion that I am the suitable candidate for that position and also will be a good partner for the team since the person writing this letter is an honest, diligent one filled with job loyalty and team spirit.

The requirement of your company is an opportunity for me, and meanwhile a challenge too. I wish to join you, devote myself to the team, and build the bright future together. Please contact me if you want to know more about me.

Thanks for your time and consideration.

Sincerely yours,

Jin Weifei

Type Nine：A Letter of Recommendation

A letter of recommendation is generally written by instructors or employers about the qualifications of the person recommended to gain admission to further his or her study in colleges or universities or to gain a position in a company. When you write a letter of recommendation, you should state the purpose of the letter and introduce the relationship between you and the applicant at the beginning, describe and elaborate the qualifications of the applicant from the perspectives of academic achievements and relevant abilities in the body, and at the end of the writing, give reassurance of the applicant's qualifications and express your appreciation for the recipient's attention to the letter.

Sample

Nov 29, 2011

Dear Coordinator of Graduate Studies:

I was asked to write a recommendation letter by Miss Shannon Chen to support her application for admission into your Program in Socialcultural Anthropology.

Miss Chen was a former student of mine at ____ University where she completed her undergraduate studies in English, and was my Student Assistant for over a year before she went to study in Whitman College (USA) as an exchange student.

I moved to ____ University this summer, and have visited her twice in Shanghai where she is completing her Graduate Studies next June.

After talks with her about her studies and future plan, I have encouraged her to pursue a doctoral degree in the USA where I got mine years ago.

Miss Chen's academic and scholastic performance over the years has been nothing but excellent as revealed in all her course scores, thanks to her understanding of the concept of modern education, her spirit of inquiry and knowing, and her largeness of mind and vision. Her dedication to academic life and her effort in striving for excellence are the powerhouse that guarantees her academic success. Besides, her writing has a philosophical depth, intellectual breadth, originality and versatility. Moreover, her ideas as expressed in papers and quick-mindedness as shown during other academic activities are executed in exquisite English. Her near-native pronunciation and fluency have contributed much to her academic success.

It was delightful and intellectually enlightening to watch her grow from a Freshman student to a conscientious and serious young scholar, who always taxes her talents to the utmost for completion and success on whatever she is assigned and determined to accomplish.

Most importantly, Miss Chen is a conscientious, and ambitious student, whose overall performance as an English major fascinates every one of her professors.

Acquaintance with her for about seven years enables me to evaluate her as a remarkably talented young lady: gentle, charming, intelligent, congenial, and helpful.

I am sure Miss Chen will bring to any program the aforementioned qualities of intellectual probity, breadth, clarity and collegiality. I recommend her without reservation.

Sincerely yours,

Dr. G. Li

Section **T**hree: Features of Letter Language

The common language features of both informal and formal letters are accuracy, brevity and clarity. However, the style and tone of a personal letter differ from those of a business letter. On the whole, the former is casual, while the latter is formal; the former is expected to be friendly and sound pleasant; the latter is supposed to be polite in tone and concise in wording; paragraphs in business letters tend to be short and focused, while paragraphs in informal letters are more likely to be long and jump from one topic to another just as a free face-to-face talk between friends.

Mini-task One: *Reading and Discussion*

Directions: Read the letters given below and analyze their respective language features in small groups.

Letter One: An Informal Letter

Sept. 18, 2011

Dear Kelly,

What's up! I haven't seen you for a long time, and I miss you very much. Last time, you told me that you had transferred to another school. How is your new school life? I guess you have made lots of friends, as you are such an enchanting girl. You have been in Canada for five years. Did you improve your English? Since you have had an opportunity to talk with foreigners, try to open your mouth and speak louder so that your English will be better.

Since I am in the 12th grade, I have a lot of homework to do every day. I am going crazy. The pressure upon us is very heavy, but we have no choice because everyone counts on us to enter an ideal college. Anyway, next summer vacation after we take the JCEE, come back to Taiwan and we'll have a wonderful vacation. We can travel around Taiwan and go anywhere we want to. I have to finish the letter. Keep in touch.

Yours sincerely,

Jadin

Letter Two: A Formal Letter

4F No. 25 Shin-wang Lane Jung-jeng Rd
Shin-juang City, Taipei County, 242
December 20, 2008

Department of Politics
National Taiwan University
No. 32 Roosevelt Road
Taipei

Dear Sirs:

I am a student in Ta-tung Senior High School. I am applying for admission to your Department of Politics. I sincerely hope that I can pass this competition after your reviewing my qualifications and self-introduction about my interests and personality. I am a person with various interests. I am fond of reading, especially those about history and literature. From them, I understand more experiences and wisdom. They also bring out my love for politics. Moreover, I enjoy traveling and taking exercise a lot because they can broaden my horizons and keep myself healthy.

During the three years of my high school life, I took part in several extracurricular activities. Among them, I liked the Culture Studying Club and English Studying Club most. In these two clubs, I gained a lot of knowledge and improved my speaking ability. More importantly, I have learned how to solve problems by cooperating with others.

I am not only optimistic, active but also persevering. I always set up a goal and exert myself to reach it. I believe that I will be an excellent student if I have the opportunity to enter your Department of Politics.

Sincerely yours,
Tony Lin

Mini-task Two: *Writing*

Directions: Suppose you are studying in the United States, and the summer vacation is drawing near. You would like to spend your time teaching Chinese during that period. Write a letter in around 150 words to the Chairman of the Department of Asian Studies of a university enquiring about teaching a summer Chinese course offered by his department. In your letter, be sure to include the following:

How you come to know about the summer Chinese course;

Why you want to teach Chinese there;

The necessary information about yourself;

The number of hours and length of period you are ready to teach.

You may also add details that you think should be included in your letter.

Mini-task Three: *Identifying Language Features*

Directions: Which phrase or type of language would you find in a formal letter? Which phrase or type of language would you find in an informal letter? Put the letter "F" next to those phrases or language types that are used in formal letters and "I" next to those used in informal letters.

I am sorry to inform you that…	Dear Tom,
phrasal verbs	Dear Ms. Smithers,
I am very grateful for…	Best wishes,
Why don't we…	Yours faithfully,
I will not be able to attend the…	I'm really sorry I…
idioms and slang	Unfortunately, we will have to postpone…
contracted verb forms like we've, I'm, etc.	We had a little bit of luck…
Give my regards to…	Our computers are used for a variety…
I look forward to hearing from you…	I use my pencil sharpener for…
Let me know as soon as…	polite phrases
short sentences	fewer passive verb forms

Look at the Phrases 1—11 and Match Them with a Purpose A—K

1. That reminds me…	A. to finish the letter
2. Why don't we…	B. to apologize
3. I'd better get going…	C. to thank the person for writing
4. Thanks for your letter…	D. to begin the letter
5. Please let me know…	E. to change the subject
6. I'm really sorry…	F. to ask for a favor
7. Love,	G. before signing the letter
8. Could you do something for me?	H. to suggest or invite
9. Write soon…	I. to ask for a reply
10. Did you know that…	J. to ask for a response
11. I'm happy to hear that…	K. to share some information

Section Four: Choice of Words and Phrases in Letter Writing

The Start

Dear Personnel Director

Dear Sir or Madam (if you don't know who you are writing to)

Dear Mr. , Mrs. , Miss or Ms. (if you know who you are writing to, and have a formal relationship with him or her—very important to use Ms. for women unless asked to use Mrs. or Miss)

Dear Frank (if the person is a close business contact or friend)

The Reference

With reference to your advertisement in the *Times*/your letter of March 23/your phone call today,...

Thank you for your letter of March 5.

The Reason for Writing

I am writing to enquire about...

apologize for...

confirm...

Requesting

Could you possibly?

I would be grateful if you could...

Agreeing to Requests

I would be delighted to...

Giving Bad News

Unfortunately...

I am afraid that...

Enclosing Documents

I am enclosing...

Please find enclosed...

Enclosed you will find...

Closing Remarks

Thank you for your help. Please contact us again if we can help in any way/there are any problems/you have any questions.

Reference to Future Contact

I look forward to hearing from you soon/meeting you next Tuesday/seeing you next Thursday.

The Finish

Yours faithfully（if you don't know the name of the person you are writing to）

Yours sincerely（if you know the name of the person you're writing to）

Best wishes/Best regards（if the person is a close business contact or friend）

Mini-task: *Writing*

Directions：Suppose you have received application materials from a Mr. Boswell, the secretary of the university you want to go to. Write a reply letter to him in about 150 words. Be sure to include the following in your reply.

Appreciating his kindness in sending the application materials；

Telling him that your university is going to support you financially；

Informing him that the necessary documents about you will be sent to him by your school soon；

Telling him what is enclosed in the letter.

You may include other relevant details you think appropriate.

Homework

Task One：Writing

Directions：Write to a friend or a family member an informal letter by focusing on one of the given suggested topics below：

1. Write a letter to a friend you haven't seen or spoken to for a long time. Tell him / her

about what you have been doing and ask them how they are doing and what they have been up to recently.

2. Write a letter to a cousin and invite him or her to your wedding. Provide some details about your future husband / wife.

3. Write a letter to a friend you know who has some problems. Ask him / her how she / he is doing and if you can help.

Task Two: Reading

Directions: Read the passages given below and summarize the writing skills for each guideline.

Passage One

Guidelines for Writing Invitations

By Janel Muyesseroglu

State the occasion, date, time, and place. Include addresses and a map if necessary. Mention if refreshments will be served. List any charges that may apply. Include a telephone number. If there is a dress code, state the preferred dress in the lower left-hand corner of the card.

If you need a response, include a self-addressed, stamped reply card or envelope with your invitation.

Express that you are looking forward to seeing the person.

Do not use abbreviations and do not use contractions (don't; we'll) except for name titles, such as Mr. , Mrs. , etc.

If dinner will be served, state two separate times: the time people can start arriving and the time dinner will be served.

If you do not want gifts, briefly state that gifts are not wanted or needed. Explain that their presence is the only gift you need.

Make sure you send your invitations out with ample advance notice.

If you have guests coming from out of town or from other countries, you may want to send out your invitation several months in advance (especially if your event takes place around a holiday.) This will allow your guests adequate time to make preparations, reservations, save money, etc.

For smaller, less formal events that include local guests or guests from nearby areas, you may only need to provide a notice few weeks in advance.

If you are inviting someone to speak at a conference, your invitation should include the following information:

Name of the conference and the sponsors;

Date, time, place of the conference and speech;

Type of audience;

The type of speech, topic, and how long the speech should be;

Any accommodations that will be made, including lodging, meals, and transportation;

The name of the contact person along with phone numbers and addresses where the person can be contacted; and

Finally, articulate your pleasure of having the person speak at the meeting or conference.

Passage Two

Guidelines for Writing Follow-Up Letters

By Janel Muyesseroglu

Mention your reason for writing the letter. Use phrases like, "I haven't heard from you, so I thought I would contact you again to see," or, "I wanted to confirm our meeting time of 2:00 p. m. on Tuesday, November 16."

If you are confirming an appointment, make sure you refer to the date, time, location and subject of the meeting.

After a job interview, it is a good idea to send a follow-up letter, as this may sway the interviewer's opinion in your favor. This letter should state how much you enjoyed the interview and how much you would like the job. Indicate that you are willing to provide additional information or references. This is also a good time to clarify anything you may have not fully discussed in the interview.

If a meeting has been scheduled several months or weeks in advance, it is a good idea to send a follow-up letter closer to the appointment date. Repeat all the necessary information, including date, time, location, and any items he or she should bring. Most importantly, indicate that you look forward to seeing the person.

Indicate if you need a response and how the person can respond to you: via phone, E-mail, in person, or by mail.

If this is a second follow-up letter, and you have not yet received a response from your original letter, include a copy of it with your new letter, or repeat the message. Emphasize the importance of his/her response.

When writing your letter, avoid negative remarks. Do not imply that the reader is thoughtless, forgetful, or negligent. If you make the reader feel defensive, they will not be likely to respond in a positive manner. Showing your frustration only makes the situation worse.

If you have sent a gift and have not received an acknowledgement, send a follow-up letter a few weeks later. Make sure you describe the item you sent. It is possible that the person did not get it, it may have been misidentified, or opened by someone else, especially if it was sent to a business.

When writing an E-mail, the letter will be a little less formal. Keep the E-mail as short as possible and stay on the one subject.

Passage Three

Guidelines for Writing Complaining

Complaining about faulty goods or bad service is never easy. Most people dislike making a fuss. But if something you have bought is faulty, you are not asking for a favor to get it put right. It is the shopkeeper's responsibility to take the complaint seriously and to replace or repair a faulty article or put right poor service, because he is the person with whom you have entered into an agreement. The manufacturer may have a part to play but that comes later.

Complaints should be made to a responsible person. Go back to the shop where you bought the goods, taking with you any receipt you may have. Ask to see the buyer in a large store. In a small store the assistant may also be the owner or you can complain directly. In a chain store ask to see the manager. If you telephone, ask the name of the person who handles your inquiry, otherwise you may never find out who deals with the complaint.

Even the bravest person finds it difficult to stand up in a group of people to complain, so if you do not want to do it in person, write a letter. Stick to the facts and keep a copy of what you have written. At this stage you should give any receipt numbers, but you should not need to give receipts or other papers to prove you bought the article. If you are not satisfied with the answer you get, or if you do not get a reply, write to the managing director of the firm, shop, or organization. Be sure to keep copies of your own letters and any you receive.

Unit Fifteen

Essay Writing

第十五单元　作文写作

要点提示：Essay 既包括说明文,也包括议论文。在英语作文练习中,逻辑推理三段论对在规定时间内组织思想观点并形成规范的文稿有很好的启示作用。由此,英语作文(essay)一般有五段,第一段是开题(introduction),主要通过对写作话题的逐步引入来提出自己的观点;二到四段是观点阐述(body paragraph),通过深入论述或细节举例来佐证自己的观点;最后一段是结语(conclusion),总结全文。

Introductory Remarks

An essay can have many purposes, but the basic structure remains the same whatever the nature of your essay is. You may be writing an essay to argue for a particular point of view or to explain the steps necessary to complete a task. In either way, your essay will have the same basic format. If you understand the significance of syllogism, you will find that the essay almost writes itself. You will be responsible only for supplying ideas which are the important part of your essay, and are the most valuable.

A **syllogism** is a kind of logical argument in which one proposition (the conclusion) is inferred from two or more others (the premises) of a certain form. "Syllogism" is used widely and the present article is concerned with this traditional use of "syllogism." A syllogism consists of three parts: the major premise, the minor premise and the conclusion.

Example A:

Major premise: All men are mortal.

Minor premise：All Greeks are men.

Conclusion：All Greeks are mortal.

Example B：

Major premise：All informative things are useful.

Minor premise：Some websites are not useful.

Conclusion：Some websites are not informative.

Warm-Up Exercises

Directions：Work out the syllogism examples as you can and read the following words to understand the logical structure in the arrangement of ideas in essay writing.

Syllogism and Three-part Essay Writing

With the inspiration of syllogism，most often effective essay writing is made up of three parts：

The **introduction** is the first paragraph of your paper. It often begins with a general statement about the topic and ends with a more specific statement of the main idea. The purpose of the introduction is to：

1. let the reader know what the topic is；

2. inform the reader about your point of view；

3. arouse the reader's curiosity so that he or she will want to read about your topic.

The **body** of an essay follows the introduction. It consists of a number of paragraphs in which you develop your ideas in detail. Remember：

1. Limit each paragraph to one main idea. (Don't try to talk about more than one idea per paragraph)；

2. Prove your points continually by using specific examples and quotations；

3. Use transition words to ensure a smooth flow of ideas from paragraph to paragraph.

The **conclusion** is the last paragraph of the paper. Its purpose is to summarize your main points by restating the main idea of the paper. Remember to leave out specific examples.

Here is the basic structure of essay writing：

Ⅰ. Introduction

Ⅱ. Main idea

    A. Sub-idea

    B. Sub-idea

        1. Supporting detail

        2. Supporting detail

        a. Fact 1

        b. Fact 2

Ⅲ. Main idea

    A. Sub-idea

    B. Sub-idea

        1. Supporting detail

        2. Supporting detail

        3. Supporting detail

    C. Sub-idea

Ⅳ. Conclusion

Section One: Introduction

The introductory part should also include the thesis statement and a mini-outline for the essay. This is where the writer grabs the reader's attention. It tells the reader what the paper is about. The last sentence of this paragraph must also include a transitional "hook" which moves the reader to the first paragraph of the body of the essay. Make sure you find a proper transition to enable you to ease off to the next paragraph.

Section Two: Body

The first paragraph of the body should include the strongest argument, the most significant example, the cleverest illustration, or an obvious beginning point. The first sentence should contain the "reverse hook" which ties in with the transitional hook at the end of the introductory paragraph. The subject of this paragraph should be in the first or second sentence. It should relate to the thesis statement in the introductory paragraph. The last sentence in this paragraph should include a transitional hook to tie into the second paragraph of the body.

The second paragraph of the body should include the second strongest argument, second most significant example, second cleverest illustration, or an obvious follow-up to the first paragraph in the body. The first sentence of this paragraph should contain the reverse hook, which ties in with the transitional hook at the end of the first paragraph of the body. The topic of this paragraph should be in the first or second sentence. It should relate to the thesis statement in the introductory paragraph. The last sentence in this paragraph should include a transitional hook to tie into the third paragraph of the body.

The third paragraph of the body should include the weakest argument, weakest example, weakest illustration, or an obvious follow-up to the second paragraph in the body. The first sentence of this paragraph should contain the reverse hook, which ties in with the transitional hook at the end of the second paragraph. The topic for this paragraph should be in the first or second sentence. This topic should relate to the thesis statement in the introductory paragraph. The last sentence in this paragraph should include a transitional concluding hook that signals the reader that this is the final major point being made in this essay. This hook also leads to the concluding paragraph.

Section Three: Conclusion

The third part is the summary paragraph. It is important to restate the thesis and three supporting ideas in an original and powerful way as this is the last chance the writer has to convince the reader of the validity of the information presented. Remember not to bring in any new ideas. This paragraph should include the following:

1. an allusion to the pattern used in the introductory paragraph;
2. a restatement of the thesis statement, using some of the original language or language that "echoes" the original language (The restatement, however, must not be a duplicate thesis statement);
3. a summary of the three main points from the body;
4. a final statement that gives the reader signals that the discussion has come to an end

(This final statement may be a "call to action" in a persuasive essay).

Section Four: Case Study

Directions: Read the given case below and understand the syllogism value in three-part essay writing.

Paragraph One

[1]Stephen King, creator of such stories as Carrie and Pet Sematary, stated that the Edgar Allan Poe stories he read as a child gave him the inspiration and instruction he needed to become the writer that he is. [2]Poe, as does Stephen King, fills the reader's imagination with the images that he wishes the reader to see, hear, and feel. [3]His use of vivid, concrete visual imagery to present both static and dynamic settings and to describe people is part of his technique. [4]Poe's short story "The Tell-Tale Heart" is a story about a young man who kills an old man who cares for him, dismembers the corpse, then goes mad when he thinks he hears the old man's heart beating beneath the floor boards under his feet as he sits and discusses the old man's absence with the police. [5]In "The Tell-Tale Heart," a careful reader can observe Poe's skillful manipulation of the senses.

The **introductory paragraph** includes a paraphrase of something said by a famous person in order to get the reader's attention. The second sentence leads up to the thesis statement in the next sentence that presents the topic of the paper to the reader and provides a mini-outline. The topic is Poe's use of visual imagery. The mini-outline tells the reader that this paper will present Poe's use of imagery in three places in his writing: (1) description of static setting; (2) description of dynamic setting; and (3) description of a person. The last sentence of the paragraph uses the words "manipulation" and "senses" as transitional hooks.

Paragraph Two

[1]The sense of sight, the primary sense, is particularly susceptible to manipulation. [2]In "The Tell-Tale Heart," Poe uses the following image to describe a static scene: "His room was as black as pitch with the thick darkness ..." Poe used the words "black," "pitch," and "thick darkness" not only to show the reader the condition of the old man's room, but also to make the reader feel the "darkness." [3]"Thick" is a word that is not usually associated with color (darkness), yet in using it, Poe stimulates the reader's sense of feeling as well as his sense of sight.

In the first sentence of the second paragraph (**first paragraph of the body**) the words "sense" and "manipulation" are used to hook into the end of the introductory paragraph. The first part of the second sentence provides the topic for this paragraph—imagery in a static scene. Then a quotation from "The Tell-Tale Heart" is presented and briefly discussed. The last sentence of this paragraph uses the expressions "sense of feeling" and "sense of sight" as hooks for leading into the third paragraph.

Paragraph Three

[1]Further on in the story, Poe uses a couple of words that cross not only the sense of sight but also the sense of feeling to describe a dynamic scene. [2]The youth in the story has been standing in the open doorway of the old man's room for a long time, waiting for just the right moment to reveal himself to the old man in order to frighten him. [3]Poe writes, "So I opened it [the lantern opening]—you cannot imagine how stealthily, stealthily—until, at length, a single dim ray, like the thread of the spider, shot from out the crevice and fell full upon the vulture eye." [4]By using the metaphor of the thread of the spider (which we all know is a creepy creature) and the word "shot," Poe almost makes the reader gasp, as surely did the old man whose one blind eye the young man describes as "the vulture eye."

The first sentence of the third paragraph (**second paragraph of the body**) uses the words "sense of sight" and "sense of feeling" to hook back into the previous paragraph. Note that in the second paragraph "feeling" comes first, and in this paragraph "sight" comes first. The first sentence also includes the topic for this paragraph—imagery in a dynamic scene. Again, a quotation is taken from the story, and it is briefly discussed. The last sentence uses the words "one blind eye" which is in the quotation. This expression provides the transitional hook for the last paragraph in the body of the paper.

Paragraph Four

[1]The reader does not know much about what the old man in this story looks like except that he has one blind eye. [2] In the second paragraph of "The Tell-Tale Heart," Poe establishes the young man's obsession with that blind eye when he writes, "He had the eye of the vulture—a pale blue eye, with a film over it." [3]This "vulture eye" is evoked over and over again in the story until the reader becomes as obsessed with it as does the young man. [4] His use of the vivid, concrete word "vulture" establishes a specific inescapable image in the mind of the reader .

In the first sentence of the fourth paragraph (**third paragraph in the body**), "one blind eye" is used that hooks into the previous paragraph. This first sentence also lets the reader know that this paragraph will deal with descriptions of people: "... what the old man looks like ...." Once again Poe is quoted and discussed. The last sentence uses the word "image" which hooks into the last paragraph. (It is less important that this paragraph has a hook since the last paragraph is going to include a summary of the body of the paper.)

Paragraph Five

[1] "Thick darkness," "thread of the spider," and "vulture eye" are three images that Poe used in "The Tell-Tale Heart" to stimulate a reader's senses. [2] Poe wanted the reader to see and feel real life. [3] He used concrete imagery rather than vague abstract words to describe settings and people. If Edgar Allan Poe was one of Stephen King's teachers, then readers of King owe a debt of gratitude to that nineteenth-century creator of horror stories.

The first sentence of the **concluding paragraph** uses the principal words from the quotations from the body. This summarizes those three paragraphs. The second and third sentences provide observations which can also be considered a summary of the paper as well as a personal opinion which was logically drawn as the result of this study. The last sentence returns to the Edgar Allan Poe—Stephen King relationship that begins this paper. In other words, the first and last paragraphs of the paper **correspond** to each other. This sentence also provides a "wrap-up" and gives the paper a sense of **completeness** and **finality**.

Homework

Directions: Choose the following essay topic that you know the most about and write a three-part paper based on the syllogism guidelines.

- The Best City in the World
- My Grandfather
- My First Teacher
- What Is the Green House Effect
- Teaching Techniques

Unit Sixteen
Summary Writing

第十六单元　摘要写作

要点提示：summary（摘要）是一种对原始文献（或文章）的基本内容进行浓缩的语义连贯的短文。summary writing（摘要写作）必须简明、确切地表述原文的重要内容。摘要写作是一种控制性的作文形式，要求学生通过阅读原文，吸收原文的文章结构与语言方面的长处，写出内容一致、结构近似、语言简洁的短文。摘要写作对培养学生善于抓住文章重点的能力有很大帮助，有利于培养学生综合概括的书面表达能力。

Introductory Remarks

A summary is a shorter version of the original. Such a simplification highlights the major points of a text, speech, film, or event. The purpose is to help the audience get the gist in a short period of time. The ability to write an effective summary might be the most important writing skill a college student should possess. You need to be able to summarize before you can be successful at most of the other kinds of writing that will be demanded of you in college. Most summary occurs as part of other essays, indeed, few essays use only one kind of writing. Generally, summary is shorter than the source but repeats its ideas in different phrases and sentences. Don't put your own opinions, ideas, or interpretations into the summary. The purpose of writing a summary is to accurately represent what the author wanted to say, not to provide a critique.

Warm-Up Exercise

Directions: Discuss with your partner and write down your understanding of your university in your own language based on the information in Website while using fewer words as possible.

Section **O**ne: **Process of Writing Summaries**

Writing a good summary demonstrates that you clearly understand a text and that you can communicate that understanding to your readers. A summary can be tricky to write at first because it's tempting to include too much or too little information. But by following our easy 8-step method, you will be able to summarize texts quickly and successfully for any class or subject.

Step One

Skim the text you are going to summarize and divide it into sections. Focus on any headings and subheadings. Also look at any bold-faced terms and make sure you understand them before you read.

Step Two

Now that you've prepared, go ahead and read the selection. Read straight through. At this point, you don't need to stop to look up anything that gives you trouble—just get a feel for the author's tone, style, and main idea.

Step Three

Reread the selection. Underline topic sentences and key facts. Label areas that you want to refer to as you write your summary. Also label areas that should be avoided because the details—though they may be interesting—are too specific. Identify areas that you do not understand and try to clarify those points.

Step Four

In Steps 1 to 3, you divided the piece into sections and located the author's main ideas and points. Now write down the main idea of each section in one well-developed sentence. Make sure that what you include in your sentences are key points, not minor details.

Step Five

Write a thesis statement. This is the key to any well-written summary. Review the sentences you wrote in Step 4. From them, you should be able to create a thesis statement that clearly communicates what the entire text was trying to achieve. If you find that you are not able to do this step, then you should go back and make sure your sentences actually addressed key points.

Step Six

Complete your summary writing with an effective structure. At this point, your first draft is virtually done. You can use the thesis statement as the introductory sentence of your summary, and your other sentences can make up the body. Make sure that they are in order. Add some transitions (*then*, *however*, *also*, *moreover*) that help with the overall structure and flow of the summary.

Step Seven

Check your writing for accuracy. Reread your summary and make certain that you have accurately represented the author's ideas and key points. Make sure that you have correctly cited anything directly quoted from the text. Also check to make sure that your text does not contain your own commentary on the piece.

Step Eight

Once you are certain that your summary is accurate, you should revise it for style, grammar, and punctuation.

Section Two: Formatting Your Summary

Introduction: The introduction part of summary writing should not offer your own opinions or evaluation of the text you are summarizing. A good summary introduction writing should contain the following:

1. A one-sentence thesis statement that sums up the main point of the source. This thesis statement is not your main point; it is the main point of your source. Usually, though, you have to write this statement rather than quote it from the source text.

2. Introduction to the text to be summarized: give the title of the source (following the citation guidelines of whatever style sheet you are using); provide the name of the author of the source; sometimes also provide background information about the author of the source or the text to be summarized.

Body: This part consists of one or more paragraphs; it should focus on paraphrasing and condensing the original piece. In your summary, be sure that you.

1. include important data but omit minor points;

2. include one or more of the author's examples or illustrations;

3. do not include your own ideas, illustrations, metaphors, or interpretations.

Conclusion: Remember that you are not writing a review. You are writing a summary. Keep your own reflections out of your summary, and aim to share information instead of opinions. When you have summarized the source text, your summary essay is finished. Do not add your own concluding paragraph unless it is specifically required.

Homework

Directions: Read the following passage and write a summary of it in about 100 words.

Despite all the current fuss and bother about the extraordinary number of ordinary illiterates who overpopulate our schools, small attention has been given to another kind of illiterate, an illiterate whose plight is, in many ways, more important, because he is more influential. This illiterate may, as often as not, be a university president, but he is typically a Ph. D., a successful professor and textbook author. The person to whom I refer is the straight-A illiterate, and the following is written in an attempt to give him equal time with his widely publicized counterpart.

The scene is my office, and I am at work, doing what must be done if one is to assist in the cure of a disease that, over the years, I have come to call straight-A illiteracy; I am interrogating; I am cross-examining; I am prying and probing for the meaning of a student's paper. The student is a college senior with a straight-A average, an extremely bright, highly articulate student who has just been awarded a coveted fellowship to one of the nation's outstanding graduate schools. He and I have been at this, have been going over his paper sentence by sentence, word by word, for an hour. "The choice of exogenous variables in relation to multi-colinearity," I hear myself reading from his paper, "is contingent upon the derivations of certain multiple correlation coefficients. " I pause to catch my breath. "Now that statement," I address the student—whom I shall call, allegorically, Mr. Bright—"that statement, Mr. Bright, what on earth does it mean?" Mr. Bright, his brow furrowed, tries mightily. Finally, with both of us combining our linguistic and imaginative resources, finally, after what seems another hour, we decode it. We decide exactly what it is that Mr. Bright is trying to say, what he really wants to say, which is: "Supply determines demand. "

Over the past decade or so, I have known many students like him, many college seniors suffering from Bright's disease. It attacks the best minds, and gradually destroys the critical faculties, making it impossible for the sufferer to detect gibberish in his own writing or in that of others. During the years of higher education it grows worse, reaching its terminal stage, typically, when its victim receives his Ph. D. Obviously, the victim of Bright's disease is no ordinary illiterate. He would never turn in a paper with misspellings or errors in punctuation; he would never use a double negative or the word "irregardless. " Nevertheless, he is illiterate, in the worst way: he is incapable of saying, in writing, simply and clearly, what he means. The ordinary illiterate—perhaps providentially protected from college and graduate school—might say: "Them people down at the shop better stock up on what our customers need, or we ain't gonna be in business long. " Not our man. Taking his cue from years of higher education, years of reading the textbooks and professional journals that are the major sources of his affliction, he writes: "The focus of concentration must rest upon objectives centered around the knowledge of customer areas so that a sophisticated awareness of those areas can serve as an entrepreneurial filter to screen what is relevant from what is irrelevant to future commitments. " For writing such gibberish he is awarded straight As on his papers (both samples quoted above were taken from papers that received As), and the opportunity to move, inexorably, toward his fellowship and eventual Ph. D.

As I have suggested, the major cause of such illiteracy is the stuff—the textbooks and professional journals—the straight-A illiterate is forced to read during his years of higher education. He learns to write gibberish by reading it, and by being taught to admire it as profundity. If he is majoring in sociology, he must grapple with such journals as the American Sociological Review, journals bulging with barbarous jargon, such as "ego-integrative action orientation" and "orientation toward improvement of the gratification-deprivation balance of the actor" (the latter of which monstrous phrases represents, to quote Malcolm Cowley, the sociologist's way of saying "the pleasure principle"). In such journals, Mr. Cowley reminds us, two things are never described as being "alike." They are "homologous" or "isomorphic." Nor are things simply "different." They are "allotropic." In such journals writers never "divide anything." They "dichotomize" or "bifurcate" things.

Unit Seventeen

Critical Essay

第 十 七 单 元　评 论 分 析

要点提示：英语的 critical 不等同于汉语的"批评"或"批判"，critical essay（评论分析）不同于说明文或议论文写作，它是针对原文进行的客观性评论或分析，尤其是正反两方面的评述。critical essay（评论分析）写作开篇虽然也要综述原文，但应避免写作者本人的情感抒发和主观发挥，坚持有理有据的评论或分析。

Introductory Remarks

A critical essay is a critique or review of another work, usually one which is arts related (i. e. book, play, movie, painting). However, the critical essay is more than just a summary of the content of the other work or your opinion of its value. It is an objective analysis of the work, examining both its positive and negative aspects.

Warm-Up Exercises

Directions: Discuss with your partner and work out a list of the similarities and differences between *pipan*（批判）in Chinese context and critic in English context.

Section One: Understanding Critical Essay

A critical essay or review begins with an analysis or exposition of the work. Each analysis should include the following points：

1. A summary of the author's point of view, including

a brief statement of the author's main idea (i. e. , thesis or theme)；

an outline of the important "facts" and lines of reasoning the author used to support the main idea；

a summary of the author's explicit or implied values；

a presentation of the author's conclusion or suggestions for action.

2. An evaluation of the author's work, including

an assessment of the "facts" presented on the basis of correctness, relevance, and whether or not pertinent facts were omitted；

an evaluation or judgment of the logical consistency of the author's argument；

an appraisal of the author's values in terms of how you feel or by an accepted standard.

Section Two: How to Write a Critical Essay

Generally speaking, the critical essay is informative and stresses the work rather than your opinion. You need to support any observations or claims you make with evidence. For this reason, in writing a critical essay, you don't use the first person. To be specific, you need to consider the following aspects while writing a good critical essay：

- The critical essay is informative；it emphasizes the literary work being studied rather than the feelings and opinions of the person writing about the literary work；in this kind of writing, all claims made about the work need to be backed up with evidence.

- The difference between feelings and facts is simple—it does not matter what you believe about a book or play or poem；what matters is what you can prove about it by drawing upon evidence found in the text itself, in biographies of the author, in critical discussions of the literary work, etc.

- Criticism does not mean you have to attack the work or the author；it simply means you are thinking critically about it, exploring it and discussing your findings.

- In many cases, you are teaching your audience something new about the text.

- The literary essay usually employs a serious and objective tone. (Sometimes, depending on your audience, it is all right to use a lighter or even humorous tone, but this is not usually the case).

- Use a "claims and evidence" approach. Be specific about the points you are making about the novel, play, poem, or essay you are discussing and back up those points with evidence that your audience will find credible and appropriate. If you want to say *The War of the Worlds* is "a novel about how men and women react in the face of annihilation, and most of them do not behave in a particularly courageous or noble manner," say it, and then find evidence that supports your claim.

- Using evidence from the text itself is often your best option. If you want to argue, "isolation drives Frankenstein's creature to become evil," back it up with events and speeches from the novel itself.

- Another form of evidence you can rely on is criticism, what other writers have claimed about the work of literature you are examining. You may treat these critics as "expert witnesses," whose ideas provide support for claims you are making about the book. In most cases, you should not simply provide a summary of what critics have said about the literary work.

- In fact, one starting point might be to look at what a critic has said about one book or poem or story and then **a**) ask if the same thing is true of another book or poem or story and **b**) ask what it means is true or not.

- Do not try to do everything. Try to do one thing well. And beware of subjects that are too broad; focus your discussion on a particular aspect of a work rather than trying to say everything that could possibly be said about it.

- Be sure your discussion is well organized. Each section should support the main idea. Each section should logically follow and lead into the sections that come before it and after it. Within each paragraph, sentences should be logically connected to one another.

- Remember that in most cases you want to keep your tone serious and objective.

- Be sure your essay is free of mechanical and stylistic errors.

- If you quote or summarize (and you will probably have to do this), be sure you follow an appropriate format (MLA format is the most common one when examining literature), and be sure you provide a properly formatted list of works cited at the end of your essay.

Section Three: Formatting Your Critical Essay

Title: An essay is an examination of a single topic. Because critical essays must back each point with solid evidence, it's much easier to focus on a single aspect of a work rather than an entire work. Remember this when choosing your essay title.

For instance, rather than trying to examine the movie "Star Wars", examine "The Use of Dialogue in Star Wars". In a critical essay, even this topic may be too broad. Narrow it further to a topic like how Yoda's odd dialogue contributes to the movie or how the voice of James Earl Jones adds to the character of Darth Vader.

Introduction: The introduction of a critical essay introduces the topic, including the name of the work that you're analyzing and the author or artist of the work. It also states your position on the work and briefly outlines the questions that lead you to develop the arguments you'll detail in the body of your essay. It is more effective for you to use relevant background or historical information to show the importance of the work and the reason for your evaluation.

Body: The body of a critical essay contains information that supports your position on the topic. Develop your arguments through using facts that explain your position, compare it to the opinions of experts, and evaluate the work. Directly follow each statement of opinion with supporting evidence.

1. The critical essay should briefly examine other opinions of the work, using them to strengthen your position. Use both the views of experts that are contrary to your viewpoint as well as those in agreement with your position.

2. Use your evidence to show why your conclusion is stronger than opposing views, examining the strength of others' reasoning and the quality of their conclusions in contrast to yours.

3. As for comparisons, include examples, statistics, and anecdotes.

4. Find supporting evidence within the work itself, in other critical discussions of the work, and through external sources such as a biography of the author or artist.

Conclusion: The conclusion of your critical essay restates your position and summarizes how your evidence supports your point of view. Remember to restate the title and author of the work in the conclusion.

Homework

Task One: Brainstorming and Writing

Directions: Choose the following critical essay topics you are interested in and familiar with to discuss and write down the key words by brainstorming.

- The Policy of Opening-up
- The Educational System of the USA
- My Favorite Movie
- Shakespeare's *The Merchant of Venice*

Task Two: *Reading and Understanding*

Directions: Read the following passages and discuss the writing skills for critical essay writing in small groups.

All Hallows' Eve

Charles Williams

Charles Williams was one of the less known members of the literature club "The Inklings," represented by such world-famous writers as C. S. Lewis and J. R. R. Tolkien. He didn't manage to achieve the same level of fame, but for a limited audience his seven novels represent a much greater treasure than even *The Lord of the Rings* and *The Chronicles of Narnia*.

At a glance, the plot of *All Hallows' Eve* resembles either a horror novel or a mystical thriller of sorts: a woman that dies in the opening scene and continues to wander the spiritual replica of London as a ghost, the apocalyptic figure of Simon LeClerk, the leader of a seemingly harmless sect who in fact is undoubtedly the Antichrist, two paintings that carry in themselves some connection with the spiritual world and change in the course of time…But a closer look eliminates this impression, showing that it is in fact a religiously philosophical novel that features very bizarre backgrounds simply for the sake of making a point in a more demonstrative manner.

Action is scarce; most of the text is devoted to the reflections, feelings, impressions of the main characters on undergoing various mystical experiences. There is no battle against the Antichrist in the manner of Hollywood movies and no superhuman powers of evil—in fact, Simon LeClerk uses some forbidden arts at several points, but his methods do not resemble what is generally understood as magic in the slightest.

All in all, *All Hallows' Eve* is a brilliant, yet undeservedly forgotten masterpiece. Being much deeper than *The Lord of the Rings*, however, it seems to have lost the battle for audience.

Unit Eighteen
MLA Style and Format

第十八单元 MLA 体例与格式

要点提示：规范意识是科学精神的基础,遵守格式要求,服从论文写作规范,是严谨的治学精神和严肃的学习态度的自然体现。MLA 的学期论文写作和研究论文写作格式规范,是目前绝大多数北美大学语言和文学学科的首选。对于英语专业以及所有使用英语写作的学生,恪守格式规范和基本标点符号使用规范是最基本的要求。比如,将逗号写在后引号外边就完全不符合英语的标点符号使用规范,而这是中国学生在英文写作时经常犯的错误。

Introductory Remarks

Awareness of format requirements and standards bespeaks the spirit of science, while effort and ability to meet the format requirements naturally demonstrates your spirit of inquiry and serious attitude toward learning itself. MLA (Modern Language Association) style is most commonly used to write papers and cite sources within the liberal arts and humanities. This unit, updated to reflect the MLA Handbook for Writers of Research Papers (7th ed.) and the MLA Style Manual and Guide to Scholarly Publishing (3rd ed.), offers examples for the general format of MLA research papers, in-text citations, and the Works Cited page. The integration of this unit to this textbook results in the realization that students and scholars alike in China often overlook the importance of this style, hence hardly any of the written presentations in English, whether it is a paper by a student or dissertations by young scholars, is found completely correct or consistent in formatting, documentation, punctuation, in-text citations, and Works Cited page. The most troubling is the usage of coma and quotation marks.

Warm-Up Exercises

Directions: Work out a list of points about the importance of following the style and format, and then discuss it in small groups.

Mini-task One: *Picking Format Errors*

Directions: Use whatever textbooks at hand to find consistence in format and style, and pay special attention to how the in-text citations are documented, and to the documentations of bibliographies or Works Cited page at the end of a book or an essay.

Mini-task Two: *Discussion*

Directions: Discuss the following questions.

1. What does research in humanities mean to you?
2. How do you usually do your research essay? And what format and style do you follow, if there is any?
3. How frustrated were you when your instructor or mentor returned your paper with comments on your errors in format and style?
4. How much do you know about MLA format and style?

Section One: What Can MLA Style Do?

Research in the humanities generally involves interpreting a text or a work of art within a historical and cultural context, making connections, exploring meaning, idea, concept, articulating issues, making arguments, and uncovering contradictions. Research in the humanities is often interdisciplinary, bridging literature and history, culture, gender, class, race, environment, philosophy or religion. Because the subject areas are harder to categorize, the terminology used in humanities research may be less solid and agreed upon than that in other fields. Researchers in the humanities are more likely to draw material from texts and artifacts than from original data gathering and experimentation. Scholars in the humanities typically use library resources in at least three ways:

- to obtain primary sources to be interpreted or analyzed
- to find secondary sources to put primary sources in a critical context
- to seek answers to specific questions that arise during research

Whatever the nature of the research, you must be prepared to use citations in relevant texts to locate other material and clarify connections among works, and you must follow MLA format and style. In other words, you must demonstrate correct use of the specifics in your written presentation.

MLA style specifies guidelines for formatting manuscripts and also provides writers with a system for referencing their sources through parenthetical citation in their essays and Works Cited pages.

What can MLA do to your paper or research essay? Nothing, but it is the formal and only acceptable way to present your ideas in writing.

Section Two: Paper Format

The preparation of papers and manuscripts in MLA style must follow the basic guidelines for formatting a paper in such a style.

General Guidelines

1. Type your paper on a computer and print it out on standard, white 8.5 x 11-inch paper.
2. Double-space the text of your paper, and use a legible font (e. g. Times New Roman). Whatever font you choose, MLA recommends that the regular and italics type styles contrast enough that they are recognizable one from another. The font size should be 12 pt.
3. Leave only one space after periods or other punctuation marks (unless otherwise instructed by your instructor).
4. Set the margins of your document to one inch on all sides.
5. Indent the first line of paragraphs one-half inch from the left margin simply by using the tab key.
6. Create a header that numbers all pages consecutively in the upper right-hand corner, one-half inch from the top and flush with the right margin.

7. Use italics throughout your essay for the titles of longer works and, only when absolutely necessary, providing emphasis.

8. If you have any endnotes, include them on a separate page before your Works Cited page. Entitle the section "Notes" (centered, unformatted).

Formatting the First Page of Your Paper

1. Do not make a title page for your paper unless specifically requested.

2. In the upper left-hand corner of the first page, list your name, your instructor's name, the course, and the date. Again, be sure to use double-spaced text.

3. Double-space again and center the title. Do not underline, italicize, or place your title in quotation marks; write the title in Title Case (standard capitalization), not in all capital letters.

4. Use quotation marks and/or italics when referring to other works in your title, just as you would in your text, for example, *Pride and Prejudice* as a Morality Novel, and Human Weariness in "A Very Old Man with Enormous Wings." The first title has a novel title (a book title) in it, therefore that title is italicized, whereas the second title has the title of a short story in it, therefore that title is put in quotation marks, for it is not a book title.

5. Double-space between the title and the first line of your paper.

6. Refer to the sample in this chapter.

Section **T**hree: **Citations**

The purpose of MLA citations, sometimes called parenthetical citations or in-text citations, is to document where you found your information and give credit to the authors for using their works. The citations refer your readers to your Works Cited page at the end of your paper. Pay special attention to placement and punctuation rules. Put your MLA citations close to the quotation, information, paraphrase, or summary you are documenting.

1. At the end of a sentence before the final punctuation:
   - Wayne Williams reports on a folk belief that going to sleep on a rug made of bearskin can relieve backache (183).

2. After the part of the sentence to which the citation applies:

- The folk belief that "sleeping on a bear rug will cure backache" (Williams 183) illustrates the magic of external objects producing results inside the body.

3. At the end of a long quotation, set off as a block, after the end punctuation with a space before the parentheses. Use the tab key twice:

   - Many baseball players are superstitious, especially pitchers. Some pitchers refuse to walk anywhere on the day of the game in the belief that every little exertion subtracts from their playing strength. One pitcher would never put on his cap until the game started and would not wear it at all on the days he did not pitch. (Gmelch 280)

Examples

1. **Author's Name in Parentheses**: • When people marry now "there is an important sense in which they don't know what they are doing" (Giddens 46).

2. **Author's Name in Discussion**: • Giddens claims that when people marry now "there is an important sense in which they don't know what they are doing" (46).

3. **General Reference**: • general reference refers to a source as a whole, to its main ideas, or to information throughout; it needs no page number.
   - Many species of animals have complex systems of communication (Bright).

4. **One Author**: Provide the author's last name in parentheses, or integrate either the full name or last name alone into the discussion:
   - According to Maureen Honey, government posters during World War II often portrayed homemakers "as vital defenders of the nation's homes" (135).

5. **Two or Three Authors**: • The item is noted in a partial list of Francis Bacon's debts from 1603 on (Jardine and Stewart 275). For three authors: (Norman, Fraser, and Jenko 209).

6. **More Than Three Authors**:
   Within parentheses, name the first author and add et al. ("and others").
   Within your discussion, use a phrase like "Chen and his colleagues point out..." or something similar. If you name all the authors in the works cited list rather than using et al., do the same in the text citation.
   - More funding would encourage creative research on complementary medicine (Chen et al. 82).

7. **More Than One Work by the Same Author**: When the list of works cited includes more than one work by an author, add a shortened form of the title to your citation.

- One writer claims that "quaintness glorifies the unassuming industriousness" in these social classes (Harris, Cute 46).

8. **Authors with the Same Name**: When authors have the same last name, identify each by first initial (or entire first name, if necessary for clarification).

   - Despite improved health information systems (J. Adams 308), medical errors continue to increase (D. Adams 1).

9. **Indirect Source**: Use qtd. in ("quoted in") to indicate when your source provides you with a quotation (or paraphrase) taken from yet another source.

   - Here, Feuch is the source of the quotation from Vitz. For Vitz, "art, especially great art, must engage all or almost all of the major capacities of the nervous system" (qtd. in Feuch 65).

10. **Two or More Sources in a Citation**: Separate sources within a citation with a semicolon.

    - Differences in the ways men and women use language can often be traced to who has power (Tanner 83-86; Tavris 97-301).

11. **Selection in Anthology**: For an easy, story, poem, or other work in an anthology, cite the work's author (not the anthology's editor), but give page numbers in the anthology.

    - According to Corry, the battle for Internet censorship has crossed party lines (112).

12. **Electronic or Other Nonprint Source**: After identifying the author or title, add numbers for the page, paragraph (par. , pars.), section (sec.), or screen (screen) if given.

    - Otherwise, no number is needed. Offspringmag summarizes current research on adolescent behavior (boynton 2).

13. **Informative Footnote or Endnote**: Use a note when you wish to comment on a source, provide background details, or supply lengthy information of use to only a few readers. Place a superscript number (raised slightly above the line of text) at a suitable point in your paper. Label the note itself with a corresponding number, and provide it as a footnote at the bottom of the page or as an endnote at the end of the paper, before the list of works cited, on a page titled "Notes."

    - [1]Before changing your eating habits or beginning an exercise program, check with your doctor.

Section Four: More about Quotations

When you directly quote the works of others in your paper, you will format quotations differently depending on their length. Below are some basic guidelines for incorporating quotations into your paper. Please note that all pages in MLA should be **double-spaced.**

1. Short Quotation

To indicate short quotations (fewer than four typed lines of prose or three lines of verse) in your text, enclose the quotation within double quotation marks. Provide the author and specific page citation (in the case of verse, provide line numbers) in the text, and include a complete reference on the Works Cited page. Punctuation marks such as periods, commas, and semicolons should appear after the parenthetical citation. Question marks and exclamation points should appear within the quotation marks if they are a part of the quoted passage but after the parenthetical citation if they are a part of your text. For example, when quoting short passages of prose, use the following examples:

- According to Foulkes's study, dreams may express "profound aspects of personality" (184).
- Is it possible that dreams may express "profound aspects of personality" (Foulkes 184)?

When making short (fewer than three lines of verse) quotations from poetry, mark breaks in short quotations of verse with a slash / at the end of each line of verse (a space should precede and follow the slash).

- Cullen concludes, "Of all the things that happened there / That's all I remember" (11-12).

2. Long Quotation (Block Quote)

For quotations that extend to more than four lines of verse or prose, place quotations in a free-standing block of text and omit quotation marks. Start the quotation on a new line, with the entire quote indented **one inch** from the left margin; maintain double-spacing. Only indent the first line of the quotation by a half inch if you are citing multiple paragraphs. Your parenthetical citation should come **after** the closing punctuation mark. When quoting verse, maintain original line breaks. (You should maintain double-spacing throughout your essay.) For example, when citing more than four lines of prose, use the following examples:

- Nelly Dean treats Heathcliff poorly and dehumanizes him throughout her narration:
  They entirely refused to have it in bed with them, or even in their room, and I had no more sense, so, I put it on the landing of the stairs, hoping it would be gone on the morrow. By chance, or else attracted by hearing his voice, it crept to Mr.

Earnshaw's door, and there he found it on quitting his chamber. Inquiries were made as to how it got there; I was obliged to confess, and in recompense for my cowardice and inhumanity was sent out of the house. (Bronte 78)

Section Five: Basic Rules of Formatting Your MLA Format Works Cited

1. Begin your Works Cited page on a separate page at the end of your research paper. It should have the same one-inch margins and last name, page number header as the rest of your paper.

2. Label the page Works Cited (do not italicize the words Works Cited or put them in quotation marks) and center the words Works Cited at the top of the page.

3. Double-space all citations, but do not skip spaces between entries.

4. Indent the second and subsequent lines of citations five spaces so that you create a hanging indent.

5. List page numbers of sources efficiently, when needed. If you refer to a journal article that appears on pages 225 through 250, list the page numbers on your Works Cited page as 225-50.

Book with One Author: Name of author inverted. *Title of book*. Place of publication: Name of publisher, Year of publication.

Example: Lipson, Charles. *Reliable Partners: How Democracies Have Made a Separate Piece*. Princeton: Princeton UP, 2003.

Book with Multiple Authors:

First author's last name, first name, and second author's full. *Title of book*. Place of publication: Name of publisher, Year of publication.

Example: Binder, Guyora, and Robert Weisberg. *Literary Criticisms of Law*. Princeton: Princeton UP, 2000.

Book with Editors:

Name of author inverted. *Title*. Ed. Editor's first name Editor's last name. Place: Pub, Year.

Example: Shakespeare, William. *Hamlet*. Ed. Barbara A. Mowat and Paul Werstine. New York: Washington Square-Pocket, 1992.

A Work in an Anthology：

Name of author inverted. "Title of work." *Title of Anthology*. Ed. Editor's first and last name. Place：Pub，Year. Pages of work.

Example：Peterson, Nancy J. "Toni Morrison：A Critical Look." *Toni Morrison：Critical and Theoretical Approaches*. Ed. Nancy Peterson. Baltimore：Johns Hopkins UP, 1997. 221-76.

Play in Textbook：Name of author inverted. "Title of Play." *Title of Textbook*. Ed. editor's name. Place：Pub，Year. Pages.

Example：Miller, Arthur. "The Crucible." *Elements of Literature*. Ed. Kathleen Daniel, et al. Austin：Holt, Rinehart and Winston, 2000. 829-87.

Encyclopedia Article：Name of author inverted. "Article title." *Title*. Edition. Date.

Example：Hernandez, Tomas. "Portugal." *The World Book*. International ed. 1999.

Periodicals：Name of author inverted. "Title of article." *Name of periodical*. Volume number or issue number (Date of publication)：Page numbers for the entire article.

Example：Beets, Nicholas. "Historical Actuality and Bodily Experience." *Humanitas* 2.1 (1966)：15-28. (2.1 means：volume 2, issue 1).

Website：Name of author inverted. *Full Title*. Publisher，Publication date. Access date URL of source.

Example：Nguyen, Stephen. *MLA Format Works Cited*. 17 Oct. 2011. 11 Feb. 2012 <http://mlaformat.org/mla-format-works-cited/>.

Newspaper Article (Print)：

Name of author inverted. "Article Title." *Name of Newspaper* Year or date of publication：Page numbers.

Example：Harris, Nicole. "Airports in the Throes of Change." *Wall Street Journal* 27 Mar. 2002：B1+.

Newspaper Article (Found on the Internet)：

Name of author inverted. "Article Title." *Name of Newspaper* Year or date of publication：Page numbers. Access date <URL>.

Example：Achen, Joel. "America's River." *Washington Post* 27 Feb. 2012：D2. <http://www.url.com/etc/etc.html>.

Magazine Article (Print)：

Name of author inverted. "Article Title." *Magazine Title* Date：Pages.

Example：Simpson, Rhonda P. "Exercising in the New Millennium：A Plan to Meet the Modern Woman's Needs." *Health and Fitness* 15 June 1995：56-61.

Magazine Article（Internet）：

Example：Name of author inverted. "Article Title." *Magazine Title* Date：Pages. Access date ＜URL＞.

Example：Brooks, David. "The Culture of Martyrdom." *Atlantic Online* June 2007. 22 Sept. 2005 ＜http：//www. url. com/etc/etc. html＞.

Scholarly Journal Article（Print）：

Name of author inverted. "Article Title." *Title of Journal* Volume（Year）：Pages.

Example：Melborne, Samuel. "Living in Iran." *Mosaic* 19（1986）：133-49.

Scholarly Journal Article（Internet）：

Name of author inverted. "Article Title." *Title of Journal* Volume（Year）：Pages. Access date ＜URL＞.

Example：Sohmer, Steve. "Opening Day at Shakespeare's Globe." *Journal of Modern Literary Studies* 3. 1（1997）. 27 May 2009 ＜http：//web. english. ufl. edu/JMLS. html＞.

ELibrary：

Example：Palmer, Aaron. "Colors and Blood：Flag Passions of the Confederate South." *History*. 2 Mar. 2005：64-6. ELibrary. ProQuest. Trabuco Hills High School Library. 3 Feb. 2004 ＜http：//elibrary. bigchalk. com/＞.

Dictionary Online：

"Word searched." *Website Title*. Created or updated date if available. Sponsoring organization of applicable. Date of access written in MLA style. ＜URL＞.

Example："Hysteria." *Bartlett's Familiar Quotations*. 2000. 25 Sept. 2006. ＜http：// education. yahoo. com/search/bfq？ p＝hysteria＞.

Section **S**ix: Adding or Omitting Words in Quotations

If you omit a word or words from a quotation, you should indicate the deleted word or words by using ellipsis marks, which are three periods（...）preceded and followed by a space. For example：

In an essay on urban legends, Jan Harold Brunvand notes that "some individuals make a point of learning every recent rumor or tale... and in a short time a lively exchange of details occurs" (78).

Please note that brackets are not needed around ellipses unless adding brackets would clarify your use of ellipses.

When omitting words from poetry quotations, use a standard three-period ellipses; however, when omitting one or more full lines of poetry, space several periods about the length of a complete line in the poem:

These beauteous forms,

Through a long absence, have not been to me

As is a landscape to a blind man's eye:

... ...

Felt in the blood, and felt along the heart;

And passing even into my purer mind,

With tranquil restoration ... (22-24, 28-30)

Section Seven: A Sample Paper in MLA

Angeli 1

Your name, the course number, the professor's name, and the date of the paper are double-spaced in 12-point, Times New Roman font. Dates in MLA are written in this order: day, month, and year.	Elizabeth L. Angeli Professor Patricia Sullivan English 624 14 December 2008

Page numbers begin on and with page 1. Type your name next to the page number so that it appears on every page.

Toward a Recovery of Nineteenth Century Farming Handbooks

While researching texts written about nineteenth century farming, I found a few authors who published books about the literature of nineteenth century farming, particularly agricultural journals, newspapers, pamphlets, and brochures. These authors often placed the farming literature they were studying into a historical context by discussing the important events in agriculture of the year in which the literature was published (see Demaree, for example). However, while these authors discuss journals, newspapers, pamphlets, and brochures, I could not find much discussion about another important source of farming knowledge: farming handbooks. My goal in this paper is to bring this source into the agricultural literature discussion by connecting three agricultural handbooks from the nineteenth century with nineteenth century agricultural history.

The introductory paragraph, or introduction, should set the context for the rest of the paper. Tell your readers why you are writing and why your topic is important.

Titles are centered and written in 12-point, Times New Roman font. The title is not bolded, underlined, or italicized.

The thesis statement usually is the last sentence of the introduction.

The thesis is a clear position that you will support and develop throughout your paper. This sentence guides or controls your paper.

To achieve this goal, I have organized my paper into four main sections, two of which have sub-sections. In the first section, I provide an account of three important events in nineteenth century agricultural history: population and technological changes, the distribution of scientific new knowledge, and farming's influence on education. In the second section, I discuss three nineteenth century farming handbooks in connection with the important events described in the first section. I end my paper with a third section that offers research questions that could be answered in future versions of this paper and

If your paper is long, you may want to write about how your paper is organized. This will help your readers follow your ideas.

conclude with a fourth section that discusses the importance of expanding this particular project. I also include an appendix after the Works Cited that contains images of the three handbooks I examined. Before I can begin the examination of the three handbooks, however, I need to provide a historical context in which the books were written, and it is to this that I now turn.

> Use personal pronouns (I, we, us, etc.) at your instructor's discretion.

> The paragraph after the B-level headers starts flush left after the headings.

HISTORICAL CONTEXT

> When using headings in MLA, title the main sections (B-level headers) in a different style font than the paper's title, e.g., in small caps.

> Headers, though not required by MLA style, help the overall structure and organization of a paper. Use them at your instructor's discretion to help your reader follow your ideas.

The nineteenth century saw many changes to daily American life with an increase in population, improved methods of transportation, developments in technology, and the rise in the importance of science. These events impacted all aspects of nineteenth century American life, most significantly those involved in slavery and the Civil War, but a large part of American life was affected, a part that is quite often taken for granted: the life of the American farmer.

> Use another style, e.g., italics, to differentiate the C-level headers from the B-level headers. The paragraph continues directly after the header.

Population and Technological Changes. One of the biggest changes, as seen in nineteenth century America's census reports, is the dramatic increase in population. The 1820 census reported that over 10 million people were living in America; of those 10 million, over 2 million were engaged in agriculture. Ten years prior to that, the 1810 census reported over 7 million people were living in the states; there was no category for people engaged in agriculture. In this ten-year time span, then, agriculture experienced significant improvements and changes that enhanced its importance in American life.

> If there is a grammatical, mechanical, or spelling error in the text you are citing, type the quote as it appears. Follow the quote with "[sic]."

One of these improvements was the developments of canals and steamboats, which allowed farmers to "sell what has previously been unsalable [sic]" and resulted in a "substantial increase in [a farmer's] ability to earn income" (Danhof 5). This improvement allowed the relations between the rural and urban populations to strengthen, resulting in an increase in trade. The urban population (defined as having over 2,500 inhabitants) in the northern states increased rapidly after 1820.[1] This increase accompanied the decrease in rural populations, as farmers who "preferred trade, transportation, or 'tinkering'" to the tasks of tending to crops and animals found great opportunities in the city (Danhof 7). Trade and transportation thus began to influence farming life significantly. Before 1820, the rural community accounted for eighty percent of consumption of farmers' goods (Hurt 127). With the improvements in transportation, twenty-five percent of farmers' products were sold for commercial gain, and by 1825, farming "became a business rather than a way of life" (Hurt 128). This business required farmers to specialize their production and caused most farmers to give "less attention to the production of surplus commodities like wheat, tobacco, pork, or beef" (Hurt 128). The increase in specialization encouraged some farmers to turn to technology to increase their production and capitalize on commercial markets (Hurt 172).

The technology farmers used around 1820 was developed from three main sources: Europe, coastal Indian tribes in America, and domestic modifications made from the first two sources' technologies. Through time, technology improved, and while some farmers clung to their time-tested technologies, others were eager to find alternatives to these technologies. These farmers often turned to current developments in Great Britain and received word of their technological improvements through firsthand knowledge by talking with immigrants and travelers. Farmers also began planning and conducting experiments, and although they lacked a truly scientific approach, these farmers engaged

---

[1] Danhof includes "Delaware, Maryland, all states north of the Potomac and Ohio rivers, Missouri, and states to its north" when referring to the northern states (11).

> Use footnotes to explain a point in your paper that does not quite fit in with the rest of the paragraph.

> In-text citations occur after the quote but before the period. The author's/authors' name/s goes/go before the page number with no comma in between.

> Insert the footnote directly after the phrase or clause to which it refers.

> Footnotes should be single-spaced.

Angeli 4

in experiments to obtain results and learn from the results. [1] Agricultural organizations were then formed to "encourage...experimentation, hear reports, observe results, and exchange critical comments" (Danhof 53). Thus, new knowledge was transmitted orally from farmer to farmer, immigrant to farmer, and traveler to farmer, which could result in the miscommunication of this new scientific knowledge. Therefore, developments were made for knowledge to be transmitted and recorded in a more permanent, credible way: by print.

The Distribution of New Knowledge. Before 1820 and prior to the new knowledge farmers were creating, farmers who wanted print information about agriculture had their choice of agricultural almanacs and even local newspapers to receive information (Danhof 54). After 1820, however, agricultural writing took more forms than almanacs and newspapers. From 1820 to 1870, agricultural periodicals were responsible for spreading new knowledge among farmers. In his published dissertation *The American Agricultural Press 1819-1860*, Albert Lowther Demaree presents a "description of the general content of [agricultural journals]" (xi). These journals began in 1819 and were written for farmers, with topics devoted to "farming, stock raising, [and] horticulture" (12). The suggested "birthdate" of American agricultural journalism is April 2, 1819 when John S. Skinner published his periodical *American Farmer* in Baltimore. Demaree writes that Skinner's periodical was the "first continuous, successful agricultural periodical in the United States" and "served as a model for hundreds of journals that succeeded it" (19). In the midst of the development of the journal, farmers began writing handbooks. Not much has been written on the handbooks' history, aside from the fact that

---

[1] For the purposes of this paper, "science" is defined as it was in nineteenth century agriculture: conducting experiments and engaging in research.

Sidebar notes:

If you delete words from the original quote, insert three ellipses with a space between and after each one.

Body paragraphs have these four elements: a transition, a topic sentence, evidence, and a brief wrap-up sentence.

Notice how this paragraph begins with a transition. The topic sentence follows the transition, and it tells readers what the paragraph is about. Direct quotes are used to support this topic sentence.

Transitions connect paragraphs and unify writing.

Notice how this paragraph ends with a brief mention of print sources and the next paragraph begins with a discussion of print information.

Titles of published works (books, journals, films, etc.) are now italicized instead of underlined.

Angeli 5

> The paragraph ends with a wrap-up sentence, "Despite the lack ...", while transitioning to the next paragraph.

C. M. Saxton & Co. in New York was the major handbook publisher. Despite the lack of information about handbooks, and as can be seen in my discussion below, these handbooks played a significant role in distributing knowledge among farmers and in educating young farmers, as I now discuss.

Farming's Influence on Education. One result of the newly circulating print information was the "need for acquiring scientific information upon which could be based a rational technology" that could "be substituted for the current diverse, empirical practices" (Danhof 69). In his 1825 book *Nature and Reason Harmonized in the Practice of Husbandry*, John Lorain begins his first chapter by stating that "[v]ery erroneous theories have been propagated" resulting in faulty farming methods (1). His words here create a framework for the rest of his book, as he offers his readers narratives of his own trials and errors and even dismisses foreign, time-tested techniques farmers had held on to:

> The knowledge we have of that very ancient and numerous nation the Chinese, as
>
> well as the very located habits and costumes of this very singular people, is in
>
> itself insufficient to teach us... (75)

His book captures the call and need for scientific experiments to develop new knowledge meant to be used in/on/with American soil, which reflects some farmers' thinking of the day.

By the 1860s, the need for this knowledge was strong enough to affect education. John Nicholson anticipated this effect in 1820 in the "Experiments" section of his book *The Farmer's Assistant; Being a Digest of All That Relates to Agriculture and the Conducting of Rural Affairs; Alphabetically Arranged and Adapted for the United States;*

Angeli 6

Use block quotes when quotations are longer than fourtyped lines.

Perhaps it would be well, if some institution were devised, and supported at the expense of the State, which would be so organized as would tend most effectually to produce a due degree of emulation among Farmers, by rewards and honorary distinctions conferred by those who, by their successful experimental efforts and improvements, should render themselves duly entitled to them.[1] (92)

Block quotes begin on a new line, are doublespaced, and are indented 0.5" from the margin. Do not use quotation marks. The citation information (author name and page number) follows the quote's end punctuation.

Part of Nicholson's hope was realized in 1837 when Michigan established their state university, specifying that "agriculture was to be an integral part of the curriculum" (Danhof 71). Not much was accomplished, however, much to the dissatisfaction of farmers, and in 1855, the state authorized a new college to be "devoted to agriculture and to be independent of the university" (Danhof 71). The government became more involved in the creation of agricultural universities in 1862 when President Lincoln passed the Morrill Land Grant College Act, which begins with this phrase: "AN ACT Donating Public Lands to the several States and Territories which may provide Colleges for the Benefit of Agriculture and Mechanic Arts [sic]." The first agricultural colleges formed under the act suffered from a lack of trained teachers and "an insufficient base of knowledge," and critics claimed that the new colleges did not meet the needs of farmers (Hurt 193).

Periods occur before the end quotation mark if the citation information is given already in the sentence.

If a source has more than two authors, use the first author's last name followed by "et al."

Congress addressed these problems with the then newly formed United States Department of Agriculture (USDA). The USDA and Morrill Act worked together to form "... State experiment stations and extension services...[that] added [to] ... localized research and education ..." (Baker et al. 415). The USDA added to the scientific and educational areas of the agricultural field in other ways by including

---

[1] Please note that any direct quotes from the nineteenth century texts are written in their original form, which may contain grammar mistakes according to twenty-first century grammar rules.

Angeli 7

research as one of the organization's "foundation stone" (367) and by including these

seven objectives:

(1) [C]ollecting, arranging, and publishing statistical and other useful agricultural

information; (2) introducing valuable plants and animals; (3) answering inquiries

of farmers regarding agriculture; (4) testing agricultural implements;

(5) conducting chemical analyses of soils, grains, fruits, plants, vegetables, and

manures; (6) establishing a professorship of botany and entomology; and

(7) establishing an agricultural library and museum. (Baker et al. 14)

These objectives were a response to farmers' needs at the time, mainly to the need for

experiments, printed distribution of new farming knowledge, and education. Isaac

Newton, the first Commissioner of Agriculture, ensured these objectives would be

realized by stressing research and education with the ultimate goal of helping farmers

improve their operations (Hurt 190).

Before the USDA assisted in the circulation of knowledge, however, farmers

wrote about their own farming methods. This brings me to my next section in which I

examine three handbooks written by farmers and connect my observations of the texts

with the discussion of agricultural history I have presented above.

Note: Sections of this essay have been deleted to shorten the length of the paper

CONCLUSION | The conclusion "wraps up" what you have been discussing in your paper.

Because this is a B-level header, the paragraph is not indented.

From examining Drown's, Allen's, and Crozier and Henderson's handbooks in light of

nineteenth century agricultural history, I can say that science and education seem to have

had a strong influence on how and why these handbooks were written. The authors' ethos

is created by how they align themselves as farmers with science and education either by

Angeli 8

The conclusion should restate the following: your topic, your topic's importance, your thesis, and your supporting points.

supporting or by criticizing them. Regardless of their stance, the authors needed to create an ethos to gain an audience, and they did this by including tables of information, illustrations of animals and buildings, reasons for educational reform, and pieces of advice to young farmers in their texts. It would be interesting to see if other farming handbooks of the same century also convey a similar ethos concerning science and education in agriculture. Recovering more handbooks in this way could lead to a better, more complete understanding of farming education, science's role in farming and education, and perhaps even an understanding of the rhetoric of farming handbooks in the nineteenth century.

You may end your conclusion with a call for action or future research possibilities. You might also include what this would add to your topic's field.

Angeli 9

The Works
Cited page
begins on a
new page.
Center the
title "Works
Cited"
without
underlining,
bolding, or
italicizing it.
If there is
only one
entry, title
this page
"Work
Cited."

The Works Cited page is a
list of all the sources cited
in your paper.

MLA now
requires all
sources to
have a
publication
marker. For
example,
books
receive the
marker
"Print"
after the
citation.

MLA no
longer
requires
URLs in the
Works
Cited.
Instead,
you must
write
"Web"
before the
date of
access in
the entry.
This serves
as the
entry's
publication
marker.

If a print
source
does not
list a
publisher
and you
can infer
who the
publisher is,
place the
publisher's
name in
brackets.

Works Cited

Allen, R. L. *The American Farm Book*; *or Compend of American Agriculture*; *Being a*
Practical Treatise on Soils, *Manures*, *Draining*, *Irrigation*, *Grasses*, *Grain*,
Roots, *Fruits*, *Cotton*, *Tobacco*, *Sugar Cane*, *Rice*, *and Every Staple Product of*
the United States with the Best Methods of Planting, *Cultivating*, *and Preparation*
for Market. New York: C. M. Saxton, 1849. Print.

Baker, Gladys L., Wayne D. Rasmussen, Vivian Wiser, and Jane M. Porter. *Century of*
Service: *The First 100 Years of the United States Department of Agriculture*.
[Federal Government], 1996. Print.

Danhof, Clarence H. Change in Agriculture: *The Northern United States*, *1820-1870*.
Cambridge, MA: Harvard UP, 1969. Print.

Demaree, Albert Lowther. *The American Agricultural Press 1819-1860*. New York:
Columbia UP, 1941. Print.

Drown, William and Solomon Drown. *Compendium of Agriculture or the Farmer's*
Guide, *in the Most Essential Parts of Husbandry and Gardening*; *Compiled from*
the Best American and European Publications, *and the Unwritten Opinions of*
Experienced Cultivators. Providence: Field & Maxcy, 1824. Print.

"Historical Census Browser." *University of Virginia Library*. 2007. Web. 6 Dec. 2008.

Hurt, R. Douglas. *American Agriculture*: *A Brief History*. Ames, IA: Iowa State UP,
1994. Print.

Lorain, John. *Nature and Reason Harmonized in the Practice of Husbandry*.
Philadelphia: H. C. Carey & I. Lea, 1825. Print.

Morrill Land Grant Act of 1862. 2003. Prairie View A&M University. Web. 6 Dec. 2008.

Nicholson, John. *The Farmer's Assistant; Being a Digest of All That Relates to*

Agriculture and the Conducting of Rural Affairs; Alphabetically Arranged and

Adapted for the United States. [Philadelphia]: Benjamin Warner, 1820. Print.

For more information on organizing your papers, visit these OWL pages:

- Argument essays: http://owl.english.purdue.edu/owl/resource/724/01/

- Exploratory essays: http://owl.english.purdue.edu/owl/resource/728/01/

References

1. Alfano, Christine L. , and Alyssa J. O'Brien. Envision: writing and researching argruments [M]. 2nd ed. London: Longman, 2006.

2. Baskoff, Florence. Guided composition [M]. Boston: Houghton Mifflin Company, 1971.

3. Bander, Robert G. From sentence to paragraph [M]. New York: Holt, Rinehart & Winston, 1980.

4. Bullock, Richard, and Maureen Daily Goggin. The Norton field guide to writing with readings [M]. New York: W. W. Norton, 2006.

5. Clouse, Barbra Fine. The student writer [M]. New York: McGraw-Hill, Inc. , 1992.

6. Coats, Sandra, and Mary Anne Sandel. Paragraph writing [M]. New Jersey: Prentice-Hall, Inc. , 1986.

7. Crusius, Timothy W. , and Carolyn E. Cannell. The aims of argument: a text and reader [M]. 5th ed. New York: McGraw-Hill, 2006.

8. Dessler, Gary. Management: leading people and organizations in the 21st century [M]. New Jersey: Prentice-Hall, 1998.

9. Faigley, Lester. Writing: a guide for college and beyond [M]. London: Longman, 2007.

10. Fennell, Francis L. Collegiate English handbook [M]. San Diego: Collegiate Press, 1991.

11. Heffernan, James A. W. , and John E. Lincoln. Writing: a college book [M]. New York: Norton & Company Inc. , 1987.

12. Herman, W. Reading, writing, rhetoric [M]. New York: Holt, Rinehart & Winston, 1987.

13. Kane, Thomas S. The Oxford guide to writing [M]. New York: Oxford UP, 1983.

14. Kirszner, Laurie G. , and Stephen R. Mandell. Patterns for college writing [M]. Boston: St. Martin's Press, 1983.

15. Lunsford, Andrea A. , John J. Ruszkiewicz & Keith Walters. Everything's an argument with readings [M]. Boston: St. Martin's Press, 2001.

16. McCrimmon, J. M. Writing with a purpose [M]. 8th ed. Boston: Houghton Mifflin Company, 1984.

17. McQuade, Donald, and Christine McQuade. Seeing & writing [M]. Boston: St. Martin's Press, 2003.

18. Ober, Scott. Contemporary business communication [M]. Boston: Houghton Mifflin Company, 1998.

19. Palmquist, Michael. The Bedford researcher [M]. 2nd ed. Boston: Bedford/St. Martin's, 2006.

20. Ramage, John D. , John C. Bean, and June Johnson. The Allyn and Bacon guide to writing [M]. 4th ed. Longman.

21. Reid, Stephen. The Prentice Hall guide for college writers [M]. New Jersey: Prentice-Hall, Inc. , 1989.

22. Rotternbertg, Annette T. Elements of argument: a text and reader [M]. New York: St. Martin's Press, 1985.